Becoming Computer-Literate

A Plain-English Guide for Lawyers and Other Legal Professionals

by Carol Woodbury, J.D.

 Section of Law Practice Management

The Section of Law Practice Management, American Bar Association, offers an educational program for lawyers in practice. Books and other materials are published in furtherance of that program. Authors and editors of publications may express their own legal interpretations and opinions, which are not necessarily those of either the American Bar Association or the Section of Law Practice Management unless adopted pursuant to the By-laws of the Association. The opinions expressed do not reflect in any way a position of the Section or the American Bar Association.

Library of Congress Catalog Card Number 94-072409
ISBN 1-57073-029-6

95 96 97 98 99 5 4 3 2 1

Discounts are available for books ordered in bulk. Special consideration is given to state bars, CLE programs, and other bar-related organizations. Inquire at Publications Planning and Marketing, American Bar Association, 750 N. Lake Shore Drive, Chicago, Illinois 60611.

Contents

Acknowledgments

Thanks to the people who reviewed the first draft of this book and gave me useful comments: Burgess Allison, Doug Dougherty, Mary Hayes, Diane Hill, Brian Duncan Howard, Jeff Miller, Gary Munneke, Bindu Reddy, Ernest Schaal, and David Vandagriff. Thanks to Jane Johnston and Carol Siedell of the ABA for their tremendous efforts in getting this book published.

Also thanks to those who provided inspiration for the ideas and examples in this book, including ABA staff members, past and present; Ray Bishop; Doug Dougherty; Jim Eidelman; Leon Harrison Register, Jr.; Marilyn Sanford Slusarski; Max Atkin Woodbury; and visitors to the ABA LawTech Center, late 1989 to early 1993.

Special thanks to Doug Dougherty and Ernie Schaal for holding my hand through the writing and revising of this manuscript.

This Book Is Dedicated to Pat Register

Foreword

The computer revolution has transformed the practice of law in ways that most lawyers could never anticipate. In fact, not too long ago computers were behemoth machines ensconced in fortified compounds in research laboratories, universities, and mammoth companies. Even in the early 1980s, only the largest law firms possessed the resources or fortitude to use computers to automate their systems. During the 1970s, dedicated word processors slowly replaced electric typewriters just as the electrics had replaced manuals a decade earlier.

In 1982, while investigating options for word processors for my office—we eventually went with Wang—a salesman visited me selling what he called a microcomputer. This machine, he said, would do word processing and a whole lot more. "How?" I wondered.

The secret, he explained, was that the machine ran programs that could be inserted into a disk drive, as opposed to incorporating the instructions in the electronic circuits of the machine itself. By using this new "software," as he called it, the owner of this computer could do almost anything. "Where will I get this 'software'?" Very soon, he proclaimed, programmers would be developing it; in the meantime, I could write my own. That was too much for me; the turnkey security of Wang sounded much more palatable than the do-it-yourself computer (I think it was called a Vector).

I have no idea what happened to that salesman, or to his company, for that matter. The microcomputer field was shortly thereafter overwhelmed by the IBM PC, a quirky operating system called DOS, and soon, a host of commercial software. I purchased my first PC in 1984, a dual disk drive beauty that is probably still running (but slowly) somewhere in the world. It took me a year to overcome my innate technophobia and sit down at the PC to learn what it could do. In time I became a reluctant but moderately proficient user. Fortunately for me, PC software appeared in the marketplace apace with my learning curve, so I never had to write my own programs. I have graduated through a series of more advanced computers to a 486 color laptop with Windows and a fax/modem, and today I can truly say that I have embraced the technology.

Nearly every lawyer can recount his or her personal introduction to computers, whether in school, in the home, or in the office. For some, the experience has been easier than for others; clearly, some are much farther along the road of understanding than others. A few oldtimers may honestly believe that they can retire before having to succumb to the revolutionaries, but most of us have accepted the fact that a new age has dawned and we had better make the best of it.

This book is intended for people like you and me. We know we need to understand the technology, but we have neither the time nor the inclination to become obsessed with it. We have a desire to know how things work without feeling compelled to solder our own motherboard to make repairs. We want to be knowledgeable enough to talk to computer snobs and salespeople without sounding ignorant. We want a guide to the technology that will explain what we need to know (but not more) in language we can understand (without being patronizing). Carol Woodbury has accomplished all this and more.

Here finally is a non-encyclopedia-length book for lawyers about computers and their applications in the law office. From her history of microcomputing, to her descriptions of hardware components, to her discussion of application software, Woodbury has produced a truly user-friendly tome. She offers her insights and opinions in a straightforward manner, and she bases her comments on personal experience in answering the questions of hundreds of people like you and me over the years.

Becoming Computer-Literate: A Plain-English Guide for Lawyers and Other Legal Professionals will be a valuable asset to you as you continue to cope with technology, and all the evidence tells us that the need to master this technology will not go away. As the millennium approaches, technology is no longer a luxury but a necessity. Computers not only permit lawyers to practice efficiently, they are increasingly necessary to permit them to practice competently. Here is a book that will help you to manage the transition to an automated age as painlessly as possible and to maximize your utilization of these now ubiquitous machines.

Professor Gary A. Munneke
Chair, LPM Publishing

Preface

"Computer literacy" is the buzzword of the '90s, but nobody seems to agree on what the term means. Some experts argue that it means understanding what computers are all about. Others argue that it means knowing how to use a computer well enough to crank out a document to give to a secretary for formatting and printing.

For our purposes, computer literacy means all of this and more. It means having a fundamental understanding of what computers can do. It means having a computer on your desk and using it effectively to do your work and organize your law practice.

Most lawyers and other legal professionals have no frame of reference from which they can proceed to become computer-literate. College computer courses don't provide it and neither do most computer books, even those purportedly for novices. This book aims to provide that frame of reference for any lawyer and other legal professional who wants to become computer-literate.

The book comes from my conversations with over one thousand lawyers and other legal professionals who visited the American Bar Association's LawTech Center during the three years I worked there. These visitors came to the LawTech Center to evaluate computer technology for their law practices, but they had no idea how or where to start. Explaining fundamental technology concepts to these visitors seemed to help them get started. After I had given variations of this brief "computer literacy" lecture so many times I could recite it in my sleep, I decided to write it down and expand it into a book.

This book presents automation solutions appropriate to solo and small firm practice, but small practice groups in larger law firms may also find these solutions useful. The book focuses on using DOS-compatible computers, Microsoft Windows, and low-end mass-market Windows-based computer software to automate law-office tasks. Much of the information in this book is "generic"—it applies to all computer users, not just lawyers and other legal professionals. These days, much of the computer hardware and software you'll find useful in a law office was developed for the mass-market.

The book is as short as it can be. While it covers the topic of computer literacy, it leaves out the "how-to's" of using word processors, DOS, or Windows, because you can buy other books on those topics later on as you need them. It does not evaluate law-office computer programs in depth, because other publications describe and evaluate these law-office programs already. This book aims to help you get more out of these law-office automation and computer "how-to" books.

The book explains computer terms informally as it goes along and includes industry jargon and slang. Informal definitions for boldfaced terms appear in the glossary. Don't expect computer terminology to be precise. Sometimes the same terms refer to different things, and you must determine what they mean from their context. For example, the term *personal computer* (PC) can mean any desktop computer, including DOS-compatible and Macintosh desktop computers. It can also mean just DOS-compatible desktop computers. Sometimes the same ideas have different names. For example, a *computer program* is also called *computer software* or a *computer application*.

This book refers to specific products as it goes along. (These product names also appear in the index.) Please don't construe any product reference in this book as an endorsement by the American Bar Association. Equivalent products are available that you might like better.

The book is a snapshot of its time, 1995, and of necessity uses current technology for its examples. This technology could be obsolete by the publication date, because the computer industry is continually creating better, faster, and more powerful desktop computer hardware and software. The aim of this book is provide a frame of reference with which to evaluate and implement new computer technology as it comes on the market.

A final note: all of the examples in the "Question and Answer" materials come from "real life."

Chapter 1

Why Should You Become Computer-Literate?

Many lawyers are unconvinced that they should become computer-literate. One reason is that the computer world is far from perfect. Computers mess up mysteriously. Even experienced users sometimes question if computers are worth the trouble. It's amazing that computer programs work at all, because they're difficult to write.

Why Be Computer-Literate?

- It will make <u>you</u> more efficient
- It will make your practice more cost-efficient
- It will help you communicate with institutions, other law firms, and with your clients
- It will help your typing
- It will make you a better writer
- It will help your record-keeping
- It will be enjoyable

Another reason is that computers aren't easy to use, even those with graphical user interfaces (GUI, pronounced "gooey"). GUIs try to make your computer screen look friendly by allowing you to display pictures of familiar objects, like the clock or the calculator in Figure 1, on your computer screen.

Figure 1

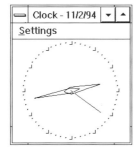

Computers without GUIs look less friendly. As a beginning computer user, what would you make of the DOS prompt in Figure 2?

Figure 2: A DOS Prompt

Becoming comfortable with computers takes practice.

Computer programs often have seemingly nonsensical requirements. For example, in the early days of the "PC Revolution," all commands to a modem had to be in uppercase. (A **modem** lets your computer communicate with another computer over telephone lines, no matter where the other computer is.) Users couldn't understand why. Wouldn't a command to a modem mean the same thing in both uppercase and lowercase? The answer then was "no." Fortunately, computers nowadays are more forgiving.

Finally, your colleagues and clients may consider technology to be low status if you depend on it instead of human assistants. For example, people often consider voice mail (or an answering machine) to be inferior to an answering service, even though voice mail can be cheaper and more informative. This point of view is changing, but people are still biased against machinery, as if it will rise up and dehumanize us all.

Ten Reasons to Become Computer-Literate

1. Because You Can

Cars, typewriters, and calculators merely help you perform tasks faster. Computers also help you perform tasks faster and, more important, computers can mimic the logical operations of your mind. They can make decisions like "If a client's account is 90 days past due, then flag it so we can call the client today."

Computers can make these decisions because they can be instructed to perform logical operations of the type "if X is true, then do Y; else do Z." Furthermore, because the computer does logic, the computer is a better typing machine than a typewriter and a better number-cruncher than a calculator—and it can search and sort instantly.

2. Cost Benefit

It's brutal but it's true: technology costs less than clerical labor does to do the same tasks. You can use technology to start a law practice without a rich relative or paying clients. If you've little money to spend, sink that money into equipment. If you can afford a human assistant, use the assistant for tasks like spell-checking court documents, keeping your computer in good shape, and getting information from clients.

3. Professional Liability Insurance

Malpractice carriers require you to keep your docket in two ways. There are only two ways: with paper and with a computer.

4. Institutions Are Automating

Institutions you deal with, such as the IRS and the courts, are automating, although some courts still refuse to accept computer-generated forms. Sooner than you think, courts will require electronically filed documents.

5. Other Law Firms and Your Clients Are Automating

Your colleagues and clients may prefer to exchange computer files with you, instead of paper files. (Files are the basic unit of electronic information; chapter 5 covers files in detail.) They may want to exchange electronic mail. (**Electronic mail**, or **e-mail**, involves sending and receiving messages from one computer to another. Depending on the electronic mail system, the computers can be in the same office or on the other side of the planet.)

Eventually computers may eliminate both telephone tag and the tedious process of sending out paper mail.

6. You Don't Type Perfectly

If you don't dictate easily, if you have illegible handwriting, or if you make typing mistakes, then computer word processing can help you. The computer will fix up your typing. For example, the paragraph below,

> copying and use of the program on the enclosed disks is is subject to the termsof the xyz lincencse agrement provided to u. u should not open this packed until you've tread the abc license agrement. by opening this packegt, you signifi that u agree to abide by the terms.

becomes, with the Microsoft Word 6.0 auto-correct, grammar checker, and spell-checker,

> Copying and use of the program on the enclosed disks is subject to the terms of the xyz corporation license agreement provided to you. You

should not open this packed until you've tread the abc corporation license agreement. By opening this packet, you signify that you agree to abide by the terms.

Obviously, the computer won't fix everything. It won't fix the mysterious transformation of "xyz corporation" into "abc" corporation. It found "packed" and "tread" acceptable. However, the computer changed "u" to "you" as instructed by Word's auto-correct function, found the "is is," corrected spelling errors, and capitalized the beginning of each sentence.

Eventually computer software may be sophisticated enough to flag "packed" and "tread" as words that are meaningless in the context of the paragraph.

7. You Don't Write Easily

A word processing program will help you write a first draft and edit it on your computer screen. You can write out your thoughts at random and organize them by moving them around on your screen. You can look for wordy phrases like "in the event of" and "in order to" and fix them on screen. With some word processors you can view your prose in outline form to check out its structure.

8. Keeping Books, Schedules, and Records by Hand Is Not Your Forte

Computers can give you a list of everything you've to do today or a year from today. Also, unless you're good at keeping paper records, it's often difficult to find what you want in them. Once you put those paper files into a computer, you can search for words and phrases in them and classify them in many ways.

9. Because It's Easier Than It Was

Several years ago PCs were ugly and boring—green screens and cryptic commands. Now GUIs have made computers more enjoyable to use. Indeed, if you're a computer novice, you have an advantage over your colleagues who have used computers for years, because you can start out with a GUI and not have to change over from the old ways.

Finally, the computer is a joy for people (like the author) who remember penmanship, long division, library stacks, card catalogs, and typing term papers as torture.

10. Becoming Computer-Literate Will Make You a Better Lawyer

If you have just started your law practice and have few clients, you have time to learn to set up and use a computer. Use this time well. Once you get more clients, you'll be too busy to experiment with your computer.

Learning and experimenting with your computer will enhance your law practice more than you can imagine. For example, you'll be able to

- get a grip on your caseload.
- keep control of your own documents and other files.
- access a huge variety of online resources.
- improve your trial preparation and presentations.

A Blueprint for Automation

Lawyers often wonder why they can't simply call an automation vendor, write a check, and get everything they need delivered, set up, and running properly. The answer is that if you could buy such a turnkey system, it would cost hundreds of thousands of dollars, it wouldn't necessarily work very well, and the vendor might go out of business before you'd finished repaying your equipment loan.

Until recently, law firms wishing to automate had no choice but to purchase such a turnkey system. Nowadays, however, inexpensive automation solutions are available. The bad news is that you'll need to be more involved in the automation process than you might like, because you need to assemble and understand hardware and software components from many different sources. The good news is that it's not that hard. Although it's far from perfect, computer technology has evolved to a point where intelligent laypersons can implement it and make it work for them.

Table 1 (pages 6-7) is a suggested "blueprint" for automating your law practice using the low cost computer technology available today. The table includes estimates of the time, money, and effort you'll have spent by the time you're done.

Table 1: A Blueprint for Automation

The Process	Relevant chapters	Estimated Time (maximum)	Estimated Cost	The Result
Read this book once through yourself, even if you plan to delegate much of the work to someone else	All	1-2 hours		An overview of what you need to do and what you'll have when you're done.
Make key decisions: (1) DOS-compatible or Macintosh? (2) If DOS-compatible, then Microsoft Windows or not?	2	Think about this for at least a few days. Ask other lawyers who've automated what they think.		These decisions will determine the hardware you'll buy and how much it will cost.
Locate computer stores in your area; request the free computer catalogs listed in chapter 4	3 (technical info.) 4 (practical info.)	1 hour		An overview of resources in your area; mail order may be your best option. Find out what training is available too.
Browse computer stores and catalogs for computer hardware; reread and use the material in this book to analyze what you find. While you're browsing, get prices on software, including word processing and spreadsheet programs.	3-4	Do this over a week or three, to get oriented and keep from being overwhelmed.		(1) A better idea of what's out there (2) At the end of this process, you should know what hardware you're going to buy, where you'll buy it, and how much it will cost.
Order computer equipment and arrange for pickup or delivery.	4	1-2 hours	$2000-$3000, depending how much you shop around	Several large boxes of computer equipment cluttering up your office
Decide where the computer should go and rearrange your desk to accommodate it; open the computer boxes; scan the manuals that come with the computer; assemble the computer.	Appendix A	Depending on how fussy you are, could take an entire afternoon. You could also have a knowledge-able friend or a consultant do it for you.		Several empty boxes and pieces of styrofoam cluttering up your office. Put these somewhere out of sight and keep them around for a few months at least. Don't throw them away!
Make sure the computer works; call the computer company's technical support if it doesn't.	Appendix A	A few minutes to several days		A computer on your desk, waiting to become useful

The Process	Relevant chapters	Estimated Time (maximum)	Estimated Cost	The Result
Start looking ahead to purchasing and using computer software	5-7 (technical info.) 8-10 (practical info.)	Start thinking about this from day one.		You should have an good overview of buying computer software and using it in your law practice.
Purchase Microsoft Windows if you have decided to use Windows software. Purchase a word processing program.	Catalogs in chapter 4	1 hour	$200-$400	Boxes of shrink-wrapped software in your office. Keep all boxes or stray paper that came with the software. Do send in the registration cards.
Install Microsoft Windows (assuming you have decided to use Windows soft-ware). Install your word processing program.	Appendix A	1-2 hours	$100-$300 for training (optional)	If you don't like the product manuals, browse for a "how to" book at a local bookstore. Now is the time to take training if it's available
Set up a structure to organize your com-puter files. You don't need to set everything up at once, just have a good idea of how you're going to do it.	5, Appendix A	2-3 hours		You will be able to find documents when you need them. You may decide to change your structure later on; that's ok.
Investigate other soft-ware; use this book, trade magazines, and material from ABA Clearinghouse as ref-erence. Once you've set up and become comfortable with your basic computer system (computer, files, and word processing), you will find adding to it easier	8-10	Over the next few weeks	Depends. You could spend hundreds, if not thousands of dollars. See the summary table at the end of chapter 9.	After word processing, start planning to automate your finances. Then decide what else you want to automate and in what order.
Explore what you can do with Windows and the word processing program: enter and print a letter to some-one. Explore other software as you buy it.	10	Varies. Try to spend at least a few hours during a time when you're not likely to be interrupted.		Get comfortable with using the computer to do your work.

Chapter 2

Strategies in the Computer Marketplace

Strategies in the Computer Marketplace

- Learn as much as you can about computers yourself, even if you're planning to depend upon someone else
- Buy products backed up by money
- Buy standard products
- Buy products that are user-friendly
- Shop around

Everyone worries about computer purchasing decisions. Will these decisions seem like good decisions a year from now, two years from now, and five years from now? Although computer equipment is inexpensive nowadays, you'll sink a lot of money into equipment, training, learning, and creating work product based on the computers you buy now.

This chapter orients you to the computer marketplace where you'll make your purchasing decisions. Chapter 11 provides a brief introduction to the PC Revolution that made the computer marketplace what it is today.

Getting Help

Finding people to help you is easy, but getting *good* advice is harder. Salespeople, friends, and consultants will give you conflicting recommendations, often without giving reasons. A lawyer who recently automated refers to a local dealer as Mr. "AllsIKnow" because he so frequently says, "All's I know is that you should get a...."

Look for computer-literate lawyers in your local bar association or in a nearby urban bar association. Many bar associations have law practice management, computer technology, or legal technology sections where you can get objective advice. Also look for local PC user groups with novice sections. Often your best source of computer help is a computer-literate spouse or friend.

You'll hear that you should hire law-office computer consultants because they're familiar with law-office requirements. However, law-office consultants often mess up and other consultants often perform well (and vice versa). You need a computer consultant who can survive in the sometimes insane atmosphere of a law-office and who is a "quick study."

Consultants and Interior Decorators

Computer consultants have much in common with interior decorators. (Both consultants and decorators will shudder at this comparison.) Both should know
- the best places to buy equipment;
- how to implement what you want cost-effectively;
- how to make deals;
- design and installation techniques;
- how to deal with defective equipment (in case the couch or the computer falls apart);
- how to deal with you without robbing you of your self-esteem.

Look for a computer consultant as you might look for an interior decorator. Check out the computer setup of a friend's office. Find out by word of mouth who does good work. Be aware that not every consultant who speaks or writes well is competent or has hands-on experience with the technology. Beware of consultants who hype the advantages of technology without informing you of the time, effort, aggravation, and money this technology will cost.

Many consultants won't tell you the basics of buying computer **hardware** (the machinery) and **software** (the instructions that run the machinery). They may assume that you don't want to know or that you're too busy to learn. Nonetheless, whether you hire a consultant or do it yourself, learn something about computers first. You know what furniture should cost, what you need, and why. You should know the same thing for computers.

Computer Trade Magazines

Computer trade magazines give good overviews of the computer marketplace and its products, but sometimes you would swear that product reviews come straight from vendor promotional materials. You can find these magazines at bookstores and on drugstore magazine racks.

Sometimes reviews ignore obvious flaws in computer hardware and software. Why? Ask any journalist who has been assailed by vendors upset that their products were unfavorably mentioned or reviewed. If you believe some vendors, anyone who doesn't like their products is crazy.

The ABA

The ABA Section of Law Practice Management (LPM) (312/988-5646) has computer interest groups for novices. Also, at this writing the ABA Legal Technology Clearinghouse is establishing a Technology Referral Service. This service will place interested parties in contact with other professionals who are knowledgeable about legal software and hardware and who are willing to share their opinion, insights, and experiences about specific products with their colleagues.

For a nominal fee, the ABA Clearinghouse (312/988-5465) sells information packets on law-office automation topics, including general automation, time/billing, docket control, and special practice areas. The packets include software lists, bibliographies, and reprints of articles from law-office automation literature.

Rules of the Computer Marketplace

Whether you get help or go it alone, the rules that follow may help you make buying decisions you'll be happy with later. If you follow these rules, you'll most likely buy products that are succeeding and will continue to succeed in the marketplace.

If you break the rules, be prepared to pay the price. The product may be hard to learn and use, expensive, or made by one small company in Timbuktu. It may be the only one of its kind. Nevertheless, the product may be worth it to you. Staying within the rules has a price, too: you may pass up an outstanding and useful product.

Rule 1. Buy products with marketing and technical dollars behind them.

If there is money behind a product, you can read about it in computer trade magazines. You'll have a good idea of what the product does and whether you need it. You can buy the product at a computer store, or you can call an 800 number and order it on your credit card. You can also call an 800 number for technical support. You won't have to wait long for the support, and the person who helps you'll be friendly, not patronizing.

Products are relatively stable and easy to use when money supports technical expertise to develop and improve them. Improvements to existing programs are called new **versions** and can include new features and **bug** fixes (correcting mistakes).

Companies can be small and still succeed in the marketplace if they're well capitalized. Indeed, small companies often have an advantage in the marketplace because they don't contain several divisions competing against each other.

Beware of companies that create, promote, develop a user base for a product, and then drop it summarily. A well-known computer software company in the Northeast has broken this rule often.

Reasons to Break Rule 1

- You contract with a small local company to write computer software that fits your needs, because you have thoroughly researched the software market and have found nothing that does what you want. This action may also end up breaking rules 2, 3, and 4.
- You buy and stick with Lotus Agenda, the first truly flexible personal information manager (PIM), because Agenda is both unique and invaluable for keeping track of miscellaneous information, even though Lotus Development Corporation abandoned the product several years ago.

Rule 2. Buy products that conform to industry standards.

The days when one company supported your computer needs from cradle to grave are gone. Try to buy products that conform to industry standards, so if your vendor goes out of business, you're not stuck with an obsolete product. A product that conforms to **industry standards** follows design rules that are well-known by computer designers and programmers.

Most industry standards are "de facto," that is, they follow a design made popular by one successful company. For example:

- The most popular desktop computers nowadays are descendants of the IBM PC/AT, an early 1980s computer introduced by IBM and quickly copied by other computer manufacturers. (When people refer to the PC, they usually mean PC/AT descendants.) When you buy a PC, you should be able to buy standard replacement parts for it from more than one manufacturer. Beware of computer companies that use expensive (and sometimes inferior) proprietary parts.

- These desktop computers are **DOS-compatible**, meaning they run (use) MS-DOS, an operating system first mass-marketed in the early 1980s by Microsoft. (An **operating system** is software that controls the computer's basic operations.)
- Most software used on desktop computers runs under the MS-DOS operating system. However, nowadays much of this software also requires Microsoft Windows, a graphical user interface (GUI), to run. A GUI significantly reduces the need to enter computer commands in a precise tedious-to-learn form.
- Today most modem manufacturers make **Hayes-compatible** modems. Hayes Microcomputer Products, Inc., manufactured modems used in desktop computers from the early 1980s on.
- Many popular desktop printers are **HP-compatible.** In the mid 1980s, Hewlett-Packard (HP) introduced quiet, fast, inexpensive laser printers that helped make DOS-compatible computers successful in the business world.
- Most word processing programs running on desktop computers can read and write word processing files created by WordPerfect, a word processor introduced to the PC world in mid-1980.
- Many database programs today can read and write database files in **dBASE-compatible** format. (A **database** is software that handles information in table form. A mailing list is a simple database.)

The rest of this book discusses these terms and products in more detail.

Reasons to Break Rule 2

- Even though the Apple Macintosh is made by only one computer manufacturer, Apple Computer, Inc., you buy a Macintosh desktop computer, because you like Macintosh software better than PC software.
- You buy a notebook-sized computer instead of a desktop computer because mobility is important to you, even though you frequently will be dependent on a single company for parts and repairs.
- You buy a Coactive Connector network so the computers in your office can share files and printers, because it is cheap and easy for novices to install, even though it is a non-standard network product.

Corollaries to Rule 2

- Manufacturers of PC hardware and software are concerned about **backward compatibility.** This means (1) new software runs on older machines, albeit slowly, and (2) new software reads and writes computer files from old software.

- Major software vendors encourage third-party development of programs that use their software. Small shops can develop these programs without a huge investment cost.
- The slogan that "nobody ever got fired for buying IBM" is obsolete. The new slogan is "anyone who buys nonstandard products ought to be fired."
- In the PC world, new products do not spring up overnight, instantly making current products obsolete. You'll have plenty of warning that a new type of product is coming on the market.

Rule 3. Buy user-friendly products.

How can you tell if a product is user-friendly? Here are a few tips:
- You understand the product's purpose and how it can help you.
- You see others using the product to do their work.
- People at your level of computer-literacy use the product.
- The product's screens make sense to you.
- You hear good reports about the product's reliability.
- Computer "hackers" find the product boring.

CompuServe, an online electronic mail and information service discussed later in this book, is a good source of informal product evaluations from end-users like you. So are other lawyers who have gone through automation.

Be skeptical of trade magazines. For example, Microsoft Windows version 3.0, the first version of Microsoft's Macintosh-like GUI, was hyped in the trade magazines. However, it crashed often and was awkward to use.

Reasons to Break Rule 3

- You buy a new, untried type of product. New types of products are often user-*un*friendly. For example, the first version of Lotus Agenda, a personal information manager, could organize information well. However, it was extraordinarily difficult to understand and use.
- You buy OS/2 by IBM, an operating system poised to supplant MS-DOS, because you're tired of the limitations of MS-DOS, you want a stable operating system on your computer, and you're prepared to spend weeks to learn it and set it up. Buying OS/2 also breaks rule 2,

the "industry standard rule," because few vendors have written OS/2 software programs yet.

- You buy a desktop publishing program, even though most of them are unnecessarily cryptic, because you don't want to depend on outside designers to put out a newsletter.
- You use a "memory manager" program to get around some of the limitations of MS-DOS, even though dealing with most memory manager software is like wrestling with alligators.
- You install a **local area network (LAN)**, because you must have fast network communication, a central computer to keep firmwide information, and sharing of expensive resources such as high-quality printers. You're willing to deal with the frustration and expense of installing and maintaining the LAN.

Rule 4. Buy inexpensive products.

If you shop around, you should be able to find a good state-of-the-art computer system that includes a monitor, a keyboard, and a good-sized hard drive for $2000 or less. A low-end (basic) **laser printer** should cost from $600 to $700. A **CD-ROM drive** (to read information from CD-ROM disks) should cost from $150 to $300. A word processing program (to create documents) should cost around $300. A spreadsheet program (to make doing complex calculations easy) should cost around $300. You may pay more for these products from some vendors, but you may not get any more out of your purchase. Often in the PC world, the more you pay, the less you get.

Reasons to Break Rule 4

- You buy a higher cost computer system because you know for certain that expeditious and reliable on-site repairs will come with it.
- New types of products are often too expensive for what they do. Right now, pen-based computers fall into that category, even though their potential is intriguing. If you're a technophile, you might buy them anyway.
- You buy a computer **monitor** (the TV-like screen that is your view of the computer's operations) that costs three times as much as most computer users pay for monitors but will be kinder to your eyes and allow you to have more documents on the screen.
- A more powerful computer will have a longer life before it becomes obsolete.

A Corollary to Rules 3 and 4

In the computer marketplace product prices fall as time goes by. Products improve as their prices go down. Companies bucking this trend find themselves upstaged by companies leading it.

Breaking All the Rules

Some legal-market software breaks all the rules. The vendor may be undercapitalized and the software maybe badly designed, badly documented, difficult to use, expensive, and badly marketed and supported. Some legal-market software requires special hardware to run. Sometimes, once you've put data (another word for electronic information) into a legal-market program, you won't be able to conveniently use it in another program.

Regardless, you can automate tasks with legal software than you cannot easily automate with mass-market software: for example, bankruptcy forms, complicated time/billing, and automatic generation of docket events.

Life in the Mainstream

Living life in the mainstream means following the four rules of the computer marketplace. Coincidentally, it also means buying what most other lawyers buy. Right now, this means you buy DOS-compatible computers, the MS-DOS operating system, and off-the-shelf software such as word processors and spreadsheets. (Off-the-shelf software means the software comes as a shrink-wrapped package available from the vendor and computer stores.) Perhaps you also buy a legal-market program to do specialized legal work. The remaining chapters in this book will present more information on these topics.

Some salespeople promise you'll be a "leading edge" law firm if you buy their product. If the product breaks the rules, you may be a "bleeding edge" law firm instead. If you follow the rules presented above, you'll have resources such as other lawyers and trade magazines to turn to when you're stuck.

Some lawyers have gone out on the bleeding edge. Their fascination with technology has led them to try products that often crash and burn. The legal community owes much to these lawyers.

Chapter 3

How Computer Hardware Works

This chapter, of necessity, describes currently available personal computer technology. But the ideas presented apply to any computer regardless of its size, including the Apple Macintosh, the Pentium, the Amiga, the Cray, and the onboard computer of the Starship *Enterprise*.

Why Is It Necessary to Know This?

You don't necessarily have to. Knowing nothing about computers, you can shop at a computer store, call a mail-order house, or hire a consultant to buy your computer for you. You may have good luck or you may regret your purchases later.

This chapter aims to improve your chances to get what you want. After you've read it, you should be able to comprehend much of what you read in computer trade magazines, computer store catalogs, or articles purportedly written for computer novices. You won't be

How Computer Hardware Works
- Learn before you shop
- Computer vs. word-processing machine
- Desktop computers
  - Processor
  - Permanent storage
    - Measures of capacity
    - Hard disks
    - Floppy disks
    - CD-ROMs
    - Tapes
  - Temporary storage (RAM)
  - Case and power supply
- Peripherals
  - Drives
  - Input/output devices
  - External/internal devices
  - Attaching peripherals
    - Drive bays
    - Ports
    - Bus slots
- Multimedia devices
- Specifications
- Mobile computers

overwhelmed by numbers and buzzwords. Overly enthusiastic salespeople and computer "gurus" may still be able to "snow" you, but they will have to work harder at it.

If you have a computer guru for a friend, get him or her to help you shop for a computer. Even with such help, the more you know about automation, the better, because an uncontrolled computer guru can set you up with a computer that can make you dependent on the guru for life.

This chapter presents the most technical information you'll encounter in this book (except for Appendix A). If you decide to skip this chapter and the next chapter on buying hardware, please make sure somebody in your office reads and understands the material.

What Makes a Computer a Computer

Unlike calculators, typewriters, and other office equipment, computers can be programmed to make logical decisions and they can store electronic information permanently. A computer is separate from the instructions that run it, so you can combine standard computer hardware with computer programs to create a computer system that will suit your needs.

A word processing machine (for which you may have paid $50,000 fifteen years ago) is not a computer under this definition. Unlike today's PCs, the machinery and the instructions for those word processing machines came as one expensive and unchangeable package. If the word processing machine went down (ceased to work) or the company went out of business, you were stuck. Many law offices are just now converting from their old dedicated word processors to PCs.

Parts of a Desktop Computer

If you have a desktop PC, ask someone knowledgeable to remove its cover so you can look inside. Ask this person to stay with you to point out the computer's parts and to keep you from doing anything you shouldn't do. Otherwise, refer to the diagram of the inside of a computer in Figure 3.

The Processor

Figure 3 shows the approximate location of the processor in most PCs. If you're looking at the inside of a real desktop computer, look for a large green piece of plastic covering most of the bottom of the case. This green plastic piece is the **motherboard** or **system board.** On the motherboard,

Figure 3: The Inside of a Computer

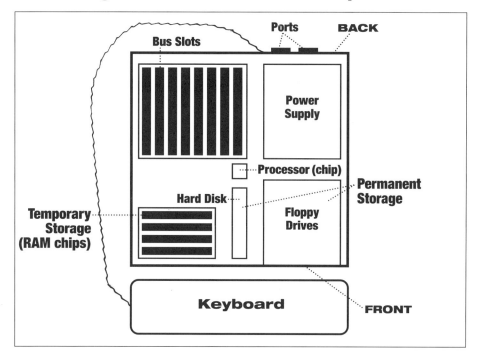

look for the processor chip, a brown chip about the size of a saltine, most likely labeled "Intel," sometimes labeled "Cyrix" or "AMD."

The **processor** is the "brain" of a computer. It does arithmetic and logic. The Westlaw and LEXIS computers perform "logical searches" on massive collections of documents, and no machine other than a computer can do them. (Does this mean that computers can "think"? Urban legend has it that Edsgar Dijkstra, a famous computer scientist, once said, "The question of whether a computer can think is no more interesting than whether a submarine can swim.")

Computers are designed around the processor. Most PCs today have Intel 80386 (386), 80486 (486) processor designs, and Pentium. Intel has had a virtual lock on the desktop processor marketplace for almost a decade.

The question "How fast is it?" is critical for processors. Processor speed is expressed in millions of cycles per second or **MegaHertz** (MHz). For example, most current computers run at least 33 MHz, while computers in the mid-1980s ran at 6 to 8 MHz.

On the horizon are Apple and IBM computers based on the new Motorola Power PC processor chip. Nobody knows whether this chip will become the new standard, eroding Intel's dominance.

Permanent Storage

Permanent storage is where your electronic information lives—your word processing documents and your computer programs, for example. Electronic information remains in permanent storage whether your computer's power is on or off.

Hard Disks

You'll keep most of your work on a hard disk. **Hard disks** are usually inside the computer. Figure 3 (page 19) shows a typical location of a hard disk inside a computer. Hard disks in today's computers usually have from 80 to 300 megabytes of storage, while hard disks in mid-1980 computers usually had from 20 to 40 megabytes.

Bytes, Kilobytes, and Megabytes

The question "How big is it?" is critical for permanent storage. Size for permanent storage is expressed as the number of characters it can hold. A **byte** of storage holds one character, such as "a," "1," or "@." A **kilobyte** (K or KB) is 1,024 bytes. A **megabyte** (MB) is 1,048,576 (2^{20}) bytes.

This book, about 33,000 words and 165,000 characters in length, took 375,000 bytes to store as a Windows word processing document. The extra 200,000 bytes are overhead. The illustrations for this book took 2 MB to store.

Floppy Disks

Floppy disks or **diskettes** are a way to get information in and out of a hard disk. You insert floppy disks into a slot in the front of your computer. Most floppy disks come in four sizes:

- 3½" high-density disks hold approximately 1.4 MB. These disks are stiff, not floppy, and fit easily into a coat or shirt pocket.
- 3½" low density disks approximately 720 KB.
- 5¼" high density disks hold approximately 1.2 MB.
- 5¼" low density disks hold approximately 360 KB. Don't buy these, even on sale. They hold too little information to be useful.

Buy both a high-density 5¼" floppy drive and a high-density 3½" floppy drive for your desktop computer. High-density drives can read both high-density and low-density disks.

Computer programs you buy off-the-shelf will come in shrink-wrapped boxes with floppy disks and a manual. The floppy disks will contain the software, and the manual will contain instructions on how to run the software. You tell the computer to install the program from the floppy disks onto the hard disk on your computer. Sometimes software comes on CD-ROM disks, described below.

CD-ROMs

CD-ROM computer disks look like audio disks but are in a different format. CD-ROM disks hold up to 660 MB of information, including statutes, case law, federal regulations, practice books, nationwide telephone directories, and encyclopedias.

Tapes

Tapes look like audio or VCR cassettes but are in a different format. Tapes are essential for backing up (making duplicate copies of) information on your hard disk.

Temporary Storage (Memory)

The processor uses **temporary storage** to work on information from permanent storage. Information in temporary storage stays there as long as the computer is turned on and is lost when the computer is turned off.

Temporary storage in desktop computers exists as **random access memory** (RAM) chips, often just called memory. If you use a memory typewriter, don't be confused. Memory in a memory typewriter is really permanent storage, because information remains in it when you turn off the typewriter.

Figure 3 (page 19) shows the approximate location of the PC's RAM. Look for some green plastic strips sitting on the motherboard. Like permanent storage, RAM size is expressed as the number of bytes (characters) that the RAM can hold. Every PC comes with at least 1 MB of RAM. Windows software requires at least 8 MB of RAM to run well. Know your computer's RAM capacity and how much it will cost to add more. Speed for RAM is expressed as access time in nanoseconds (ns). The lower the number, the faster the RAM.

Why do computer designers bother with temporary storage? Why not just have a processor and permanent storage? A partial answer is that permanent storage is slower to access than temporary storage. Also, processors can only access a small area of storage directly.

A **memory cache** (pronounced "cash") sits between RAM and the processor to make computing even faster. Most computers come with a cache from 64 KB to 256 KB.

Figure 4:
Information Flow in a Computer

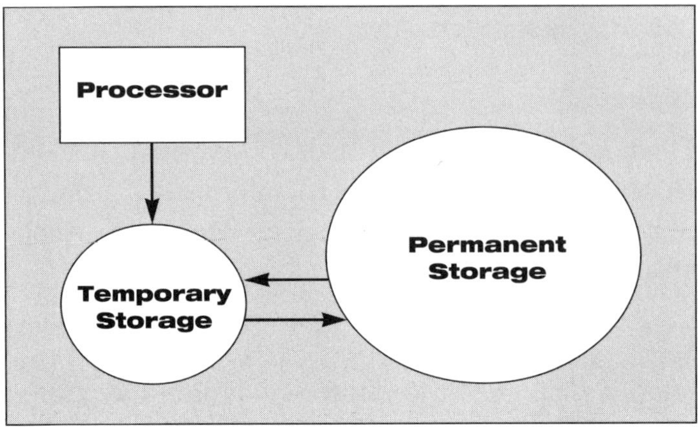

Information Flow

Figure 4 shows how information flows in a computer: from permanent storage to temporary storage, where the processor acts on it, and back to permanent storage.

The Case and the Power Supply

Computer cases or boxes (the outside of the computer) come in several sizes. Tower cases are about 7″ to 8″ wide, 16″ deep, and 16-24″ tall; the narrow part of the case sits on the floor. For desktop cases, the wide part of the case is its bottom. Desktop cases are usually full-sized, about 16″ wide, 15″ deep, and 6″ to 7′ tall), but they can be smaller (slightly smaller width and depth, 3″ to 4″ tall.) Tower cases are better but more expensive than desktop cases.

Computer cases come with a power supply, which should be powerful enough to run the computer and its devices. A good power supply specification is 250 watts. The Federal Environmental Protection Agency sponsors a voluntary "Energy Star Certification" program, designed to reduce PC power consumption to 60 watts. Energy Star Certified computers are also known as green computers.

Desktop Computer Peripherals

Hardware devices, often called **peripherals,** get information in and out of computers. Drives, which read and write to the forms of permanent storage described above, are one type of peripheral. Other types of peripherals include keyboards, mice, printers, monitors, optical scanners, and modems.

Drives

Drives are the "housing" for the forms of permanent storage described above. Hard disks are housed in hard disk drives, floppy disks in floppy drives, CD-ROM disks in CD-ROM drives, and magnetic tapes in tape drives. A hard disk and a hard disk drive usually come as one unit, while drives for floppies, CD-ROMs, and tapes are separate from the permanent storage itself. For example, you can have one floppy drive and hundreds of floppy disks that the floppy drive can read, one floppy at a time.

Most drives are **direct access,** which means the drive can directly reach any part of the permanent storage in the drive. However, tape drives are sequential access drives. Sequential access means that a tape drive must search a tape from beginning to end to find the information it wants. Sequential access means tape drives are slow (but tape storage is cheap).

Question. Several years ago, a lawyer got a new computer. On his first day of using it he turned on the power to the computer, started up his word processor, and went to work. By the end of the day, he had composed a fine brief. He then turned his computer off and went home. The next morning, the lawyer turned on his computer, started his word processor, but his brief was not on the screen where he had left it the night before. Why?

Answer. When you put information into a computer, you're putting it in temporary storage. The contents of temporary storage are lost when the computer's power is turned off. When the lawyer typed in his brief, he did not copy his work from temporary storage to permanent storage before he turned off his computer. In short, the lawyer had not "saved his work."

So many people made this mistake in the early years of the PC Revolution that vendors soon made word processing programs smart enough to save work automatically whether a human told them to or not. Nevertheless, understanding how a computer processes information will help you avoid making similar mistakes with other software that is not so forgiving.

The question "How fast does it go?" is critical for drives. It is also of particular concern to lawyers, because lawyers work with documents, some of them quite large. Reading information from and writing information to permanent storage needs to be quick, so you won't fall asleep while you're working on your files.

Speed for direct access to permanent storage is expressed as **access time** in milliseconds (ms), the average time it takes a drive to get to the information it's looking for in storage. *The lower the access time, the faster the drive.*

Hard drives today have access times of around 12 ms, while the hard drive of the original IBM PC-XT (circa 1984) had an access time of 300 ms. In comparison with today's hard drives, CD-ROM drives are relatively slow. CD-ROMs today have 150 to 300 ms access time.

Transfer rate (how fast a device transfers data to the computer) also is important for slower devices such as CD-ROM. CD-ROM drives normally transfer data at 150 KB per second. Double-, triple-, and quad-spin drives double, triple, and quadruple the 150 KB transfer rate respectively, but have no effect on access time. Today's hard disks transfer data at 500 KB to 2 MB per second.

> **Question.** The corporate law department of a major computer hardware company wants to go paperless. Money for computer equipment is not a problem. How can this company make sure the documents scanned into the computer will never be changed?
>
> **Answer.** The company can use a WORM "Write Once, Read Many" **optical disk drive.** You can only record on a WORM drive once.
>
> Third-party service companies will also prepare CD-ROM disks to store these documents.

You can read from and write to floppy disks, hard disks, and magnetic tapes, but you can only read from CD-ROM disks and WORM drives, described in the box.

Other Desktop Peripherals

Input devices such as keyboards and optical scanners put information into a computer. **Output devices** such as monitors and printers get information out of a computer. **Input/output** devices such as disk drives and tape drives do both.

External devices are mostly outside the computer and usually connect to a place in the back of the computer. **Internal devices** are completely inside the computer.

A device such as a scanner or a printer is often a small special-purpose computer because it has its own processor and memory.

How Peripherals Are Attached to Computers

When you buy a computer peripheral device, make sure you know how the device is attached to the computer and whether your computer has a place for it.

Drive Bays

Permanent storage devices such as internal floppy drives, tape drives, and internal CD-ROM drives usually are inserted into **drive bays** that have slots in the front of the computer. You insert a floppy disk, tape, or CD-ROM disk in the slot for the appropriate bay (Figure 3). Hard disk drives go in drive bays that are completely inside the computer. When you buy a permanent storage device, make sure you have a free drive bay to put it in.

Ports

A **port** is a socket on the back of a computer. Computers usually have one parallel and two serial ports. The parallel port connects to a printer via a parallel cable. Serial ports usually connect to devices such as a serial mouse, an external modem, or a small label printer via a serial cable. (Appendix A, Tending to Your Computer, contains more information about cables.)

When you buy devices that use ports, make sure you've enough ports to go around. (You can add extra serial ports to a computer by putting a serial board in a bus slot.)

Bus Slots

Some devices come with green plastic cards (also called boards) that you insert into the slots of the **bus** on the motherboard (Figure 3). Optical scanners, bus mice, hard disk drives, internal modems, external CD-ROM drives, and monitors work this way.

Computers come with six or eight slots on the motherboard. These slots should accept AT-compatible cards. When you buy devices that use bus slots, make sure you have enough slots on your motherboard to go around.

Size

Tower cases and full-sized desktop cases come with eight bus slots, at least three drive bays with slots, and at least two drive bays inside the machine. Smaller computers often come with only six bus slots, two drive bays with slots, and one drive bay inside the machine. These smaller computers look elegant and take up less room on your desk, but their design limits the number of devices you can connect to them.

Multimedia

The computer term **multimedia** can mean devices capable of displaying pictures, either still or animated, and producing sound. Examples include

- sophisticated high-resolution monitors;
- sound boards;
- CD-ROM drives.

Multimedia can also mean software that is capable of taking advantage of these devices, such as the Microsoft video clips library and Compton's Encyclopedia with pictures and sound. A multimedia computer can means computer powerful enough to run these devices and programs effectively.

Buy so-called multimedia devices when you need them. Don't buy a computer advertised as "multimedia" unless you can use the multimedia devices on the computer right away. You can buy these devices separately from the computer, and they'll only get better and cheaper as time goes by.

The time is coming when anybody can create a multimedia presentation in-house, without having to hire an expensive outside service. The days of "do-it-yourself" multimedia jury presentations aren't that far off.

Summary of Desktop Computer Specifications

A few computer companies make some of their own components. Most computer manufacturers—whether they're large companies or individuals who assemble and sell computers out of a garage—buy standard computer components from OEMs (Original Equipment Manufacturers). **OEM** equipment includes motherboards, memory, cases, and peripherals. Standard computer parts usually "come from the same vat," meaning only a few companies manufacture them. These companies are usually in the Far East.

Each of these OEM components should be compatible with the other components of a computer. For example, slow memory or a slow hard disk will hold back a fast processor. Computer manufacturers build computers with these compatibility requirements in mind.

The reputation of a computer manufacturer comes from
- its marketing efforts;
- the reliability and availability of technical support;
- its price (profit margins are slim);
- the quality and compatibility of parts.

Table 2 (pages 28-30) summarizes typical component specifications of desktop computers.

An Advertisement for a Desktop Computer from a Computer Catalog

A computer catalog from a well-known mail-order house contains the following advertisement for a low-end desktop computer.

> NEC Powermate. 486es Series. I486DX/33 ◆ 4 MB RAM ◆ 170MB HD ◆ 1.44 MB 3.5" Floppy Drive ◆ 1 Open 5.25" External Device Bay (3) ◆ 16 Bit Expansion Slots ◆ Pre-installed MS DOS V6.X, Windows 3.1 ◆ Integrated High-Performance Local Bus ◆ 1 MB Video Memory supports 24-bit True Color, Maximum Display Resolution: 1024 x 768 at 72Hz, 256 colors ◆ 3 Year Warranty (1st Year On-Site) Monitor Sold Separately ◆ Energy Star Certified. Price: $1129.54.

Table 3 (page 31) analyzes the specifications in this advertisement. Consider making a similar chart for any computer you're serious about buying.

Portable Computers

Portable computers include notebook computers and subnotebook computers. In principle, portable computers work the same way as desktop computers, only they come in one piece that you can't take apart yourself. **Notebook computers** are about the size of a medium-sized notebook and weigh 5 to 8 pounds. **Subnotebook computers** are thinner, weigh 3 to 4 pounds, and are less powerful than notebook computers. Notebook computers can run Windows programs as well as desktop computers, but subnotebook computers cannot.

Portable computers are convenient but problematic. For example, parts are often proprietary; one name-brand computer manufacturer sells additional memory for its notebook computers at outrageous prices. You can't buy this memory anywhere else.

(continued on page 32)

Table 2:
Desktop Computer Components

Part	What does it do?	How "big" is it?	How fast is it?	Comments	Brand names (a noninclusive list)	Price Range
Processor	The brain of the computer	32-bit	66 MHz	Most motherboards today have "ISA" designs; some have "EISA" designs. Some newer computers have "Integrated Local Bus" designs instead. Any of these designs is OK.		Motherboards $200-$600; cases $100-$300
RAM	Temporary storage	4 to 32 MB	70 ns access time*	RAM comes as "SIMM modules"		$50 per megabyte
Memory cache	Temporary storage	128 KB to 256 KB				
Hard drive	Permanent storage	Holds 300 MB hard disk	12 ms access time*	(IDE drives are most prevalent, but SCSI drives are becoming popular.)	Seagate, Conner	$100-$500
Floppy drive	Permanent storage	Reads floppy disks, which can hold from 360K up to 1.4 MB, depending on size and density		Come as 5-1/2", 3-1/2", high density, low density		$50-$100
Tape drive	Permanent storage	Reads tapes, which typically hold from 20 to 250 MB.		Some external tape drives connect to the parallel port and can be easily moved from one computer to another.	Colorado, Conner	$200-$400
CD-ROM drive	Permanent storage	Reads CD-ROM disks, which hold up to 650 MB	150 ms access time*	SCSI drives are the standard.	Sony, NEC, Toshiba	$200-$500

* The lower the number, the faster the speed

Part	What does it do?	How "big" is it?	How fast is it?	Comments	Brand names (a noninclusive list)	Price Range
SVGA color monitor	A display screen. Some computers require separate "graphics" cards.	Monitor displays consist of tiny dots, called pixels. Good monitors can display 1024 x 768 pixels (far more than 1000 points of light) in 256 colors. The pixels have .28 dot pitch. (The lower the dot pitch, the better the resolution.)	72 Hz Horizontal Refresh Rate	"Noninterlaced" monitors do not "flicker" and thus are easier on the eyes than "interlaced" monitors.	NEC, Sony, Panasonic, Portrait	$150-$2000
Graphics card	Goes with the color monitor.	1 MB RAM		Some computers come with a graphics "chip" on the mother-board instead of a graphics card.	Boca, Hercules, Orchid	$100-$300
Keyboard	With a keyboard you type characters directly into the computer. You tell the computer what to do by entering commands from the keyboard.	101 keys			Fujitsu, Northgate, Keytronic	$50-$150
Mouse	Using a keyboard to move around a computer screen is like taking a bus to get from Boston to L.A. Using a mouse is like flying from Boston to L.A.				Microsoft, Logitech	$50-$100
Laser printer	Prints information from the computer.	1-2 MB RAM 300-1200 dots per inch (dpi) resolution. The higher the dpi, the better the resolution.	Number of pages per minute it will print: e.g. 8 pages per minute (PPM)	Laser printers work like photocopy machines. HP-compatible is the standard. (The output from "LED" printers looks like laser printer output.)	Hewlett-Packard, Okidata, Epson	$600-$3000

Part	What does it do?	How "big" is it?	How fast is it?	Comments	Brand names (a noninclusive list)	Price Range
Inkjet printer	Prints information from the computer.	300 dpi	4 PPM	Ink jet printers spray ink onto paper. Ink jet print quality is acceptable but laser printing quality is better.	Hewlett-Packard, Epson	$300-$500
Dot-matrix printer		300 dpi	4 PPM	These printers are noisy but replacement cartridges are cheaper than laser and inkjet cartridges.	Panasonic, Epson, Okidata	$100-$300
Modem	Processes electronic information going over telephone lines. A modem device enables you to access the LEXIS and Westlaw computers far away.		14400 or 28800 BPS	Hayes-compatible is the standard.	Hayes, Practical Peripherals, US Robotics	$100-$300
Fax modem	Same as a modem, also sends and receives electronic faxes.		14400 BPS		Intel, Hayes, Practical Peripherals	$100-$300
Optical Scanner	Recognizes typing and pictures on paper. Converts this information to electronic form.	400 dpi		Scanners use the same technology as laser printers and copiers.	Hewlett-Packard, Canon, Epson	$1000-$3000
Voice recognition device	Recognizes spoken words and converts them to electronic form.				Dragon Dictate, Kurzweil	$2500
Sound board	Replays sounds such as your recorded human voice or music.			Requires audio speakers and a microphone.	Sound Blaster	$100-$300

Table 3:
Catalog Advertisement for a Desktop Computer

Specification	Chapter 3 Reference	Comments
NEC Powermate 486es Series		Manufacturer and brand name.
I486DX/33	Processor	This computer has a 486 processor, is not an SX computer (good), and runs at 33 MHz.
8 MB RAM	Temporary storage	8 MB of RAM is the absolute minimum you should buy if you plan to run Windows software, and 16 MB is better. This advertisement does not specify the total RAM capacity of the computer. Ask the dealer to make sure you can add more RAM.
170 MB HD	Permanent storage	A 170 MB hard disk is the smallest you should buy if you plan to run Windows software. Can you add another hard drive later? Ask the dealer to make sure.
1.44 MB 3.5" Floppy Drive	Permanent storage	Good, but where's the 5-1/4" floppy drive?
1 Open 5.25" External Device Bay	Permanent storage	You have a place to put a 5-1/4" floppy drive or an internal CD-ROM drive. What if you want both?
(3) 16 Bit Expansion Slots	Devices	How many slots total? Are these slots free for additional hardware devices? Probably, but ask the vendor to make sure.
Pre-installed MS DOS V6.X, Windows 3.1	Operating systems	Good if you want to use Microsoft Windows. Also good that other software is not bundled into the price of the computer—most software bundled that way has limited features.
Integrated High-Performance Local Bus	Table 2, Processors	O.K.
1 MB Video Memory supports 24-bit True Color, Maximum Display Resolution: 1024 x 768 at 72Hz, 256 colors	Devices	This sounds like the graphics capability is built into the motherboard instead of on a separate card. This is a pretty good graphics configuration, but what if you want something better?
3 Year Warranty (1st Year On-Site)		Good, but this computer is barely state-of-the-art now and will be obsolete in a year or two (but usable for several years anyway).
Monitor Sold Separately	Devices	Good—this advertisement lets you know this up front. You can get as nice a monitor as you want—you're not stuck with the monitor bundled into the price of the computer. However, the picture accompanying this ad showed a monitor, a keyboard, and a mouse. The specifications say "no monitor." What about the keyboard? The mouse? That's an extra $100 to $200 right there.
Energy Star Certified	Power Supply	Good, and does not add to the cost of the computer.
Price $1129.54		Expect to pay at least an additional $200 for 4 more MB of RAM, $60 for a 5-1/4" floppy drive, $200 for keyboard and mouse, and $300 for a color monitor. Add $250 for an external CD-ROM drive and $225 for a fast fax modem.

(continued from page 27)

Portable computers often are difficult to upgrade (to add new or better parts). For example, if you buy a portable computer with an nonremovable 80-MB hard disk, you are, in effect, stuck with that 80-MB hard disk for as long as you use the computer.

A consortium of portable computer manufacturers has created a "de jure" standard, called *PCMCIA*, to solve the problem of closed-end designs. A **PCMCIA card** is a removable card that can hold memory, modems, fax/modems, and hard disks. However, not all portable computers can use PCMCIA cards, and not all PCMCIA-enabled portable computers can read all PCMCIA cards.

If possible, check out portable computers at a local computer store. Check out the screen—can you read it easily? Take it outside if the salesperson will let you. Will you be able to use the portable computer on your patio? In your car? (One computer expert recommends putting in at least 45 minutes of heavy typing on a portable computer before you buy it. In a computer showroom, this is not always easy.)

Check out the keyboard carefully. How noisy is it? Will you be able to type notes to yourself in the courtroom? In the law library? On an airplane next to a sleeping seatmate? Check out the built-in mouse. Can you use it for more than 10 minutes without going crazy?

Check out the individual keys. Where is the backspace key? Is the ENTER key large enough for your little finger to find? Look for separate **cursor keys,** the keys that let you move around the screen. There should be separate keys for each of the four arrow keys, page up, page down, home, end, insert, and delete.

Buy a portable computer if you can afford only one computer and you want to use that computer both at the office and at home. To make viewing the screen and typing easier, put a color monitor and keyboard in your office to attach to the notebook computer. If you're concerned about office security, take the portable computer with you when you leave the office. However, a portable computer can quickly become a heavy load when you're lugging it around town.

An Advertisement for a Notebook Computer from a Computer Catalog

The catalog referred to above also contains the following advertisement for a notebook computer:

Epson ActionNote 4SLC2-50. 486SLC2/50 ◆ 4MB RAM Expandable to 8MB ◆ 180MB Hard Drive ◆ 2400 Data/9600 Fax Modem built-in ◆ WinFax Lite and BitCom Software Pre-Loaded ◆ 5.5Lbs ◆ 10" Diagonal Backlit VGA Monochrome Display, Max. Res. 640x480, 32 Gray Shades, External Monitor Supported @ 640x480 ◆ Parallel, 2 Serial, VGA and PS/2 Ports ◆ DOS 6.2 and Windows 3.1 Pre-Loaded ◆ Logitech Trackball ◆ 1 Year On-Site Warranty ◆ Price:$1738.96

Table 4 analyzes the specifications in this advertisement.

Table 4:		
Catalog Advertisement For A Notebook Computer		
Specification	Chapter 3 Reference	Comments
Epson ActionNote 4SLC2-50		Manufacturer and brand name.
486SLC2/50	Processor	This computer has a 486 processor, appears to be an SX (common for low-end notebook computers—it means the chip's math coprocessor is missing), and runs at 50 MHz.
4MB RAM Expandable to 8MB	Temporary storage	This advertisement does specify the total RAM capacity of the computer.
180 MB hard drive	Permanent storage	Good.
2400 Data/9600 Fax Modem built-in	Devices	2400 BPS is *very* slow nowadays.
WinFax Lite and BitCom Software Pre-Loaded	Chapter 9, Online Services/Communications	
5.5 lbs		Does this include the battery? Ask. A battery can add one to two pounds to the weight of the computer.
10" Diagonal Backlit VGA Monochrome Display, Max. Res. 640x480, 32 Gray Shades, External Monitor Supported @ 640x480	Devices	This is a nice size. Many notebook screens are 7" to 8" (measured diagonally). Desktop monitors are usually at least 14". If you hook up a desktop monitor to this notebook computer, your display will be low-end. Don't bother to buy a monitor that can display anything better.
Parallel, 2 Serial, VGA and PS/2 Ports	Devices	Good. You can hook up a printer, a mouse, a monitor, and 2 more serial devices to this computer.
DOS 6.2 and Windows 3.1 Pre-Loaded	Operating Systems	
Logitech Trackball	Devices	This is a type of pointing device. It's not a mouse, exactly; it's more like a ball you roll under your thumb. Some people like it, some don't.
1 Year On-Site Warranty		
What's missing in these specifications?		How many keys on the keyboard? Does it have a 3.5" floppy drive built in?

Growth in the Computer Industry

The computer industry stays alive by creating increasingly powerful computer hardware and by writing computer software that strains the limits of this hardware. To be fair, software development is a long process. Software publishers must design software for equipment that will come to market years after software development has begun.

Tables 5 and 6 show typical specifications for the earliest PCs and for PCs popular in 1994.

<table>
<tr><td colspan="8" align="center">**Table 5:**
Typical Specifications for Computer Parts</td></tr>
<tr><td>Model</td><td>Year</td><td>Processor Type</td><td>Processor Speed</td><td>Hard Disk Size</td><td>Hard Disk Speed*</td><td>Total Memory Size</td><td>Memory Speed</td></tr>
<tr><td>IBM PC XT</td><td>1984</td><td>8088</td><td>4.77 MHz</td><td>10 MB</td><td>85 ms*</td><td>640 KB</td><td>200 ns*</td></tr>
<tr><td>IBM AT</td><td>1986</td><td>80286</td><td>8 MHz</td><td>40 MB</td><td>35 ms*</td><td>640 KB</td><td>150 ns*</td></tr>
<tr><td>1994 PCs</td><td>1994</td><td>80386 80486</td><td>66 MHz</td><td>300 MB</td><td>12 ms*</td><td>16 MB</td><td>70 ns*</td></tr>
</table>

The lower the number, the higher the speed.

<table>
<tr><td colspan="4" align="center">**Table 6:**
Typical Specifications for
Computer Devices</td></tr>
<tr><td>Year</td><td>Modem</td><td>Monitor</td><td>Printer, dots per inch (dpi)</td></tr>
<tr><td>1984</td><td>300 BPS</td><td>Monochrome</td><td>Dot matrix, 150 dpi</td></tr>
<tr><td>1986</td><td>1200 BPS</td><td>Monochrome</td><td>Laser printer, 300 dpi</td></tr>
<tr><td>1994</td><td>14400 BPS</td><td>SVGA color</td><td>Laser printer, 600 dpi</td></tr>
</table>

Chapter 4

Buying a Computer

Buying a computer
- A cost-effective PC system
  - Optional equipment
  - Printers
  - Mobile computers
- Learning about new equipment
- Money considerations
- Equipment sources
- Precautions
  - About specifications
  - About advertisements

Computers are consumer products. It doesn't matter whether you're a lawyer, a doctor, an accountant, or a computer programmer. You buy computers where everybody else does: a local dealer, a computer discount store, or a mail-order house.

Cost-Effective Desktop Computer Systems

A cost-effective desktop computer will run state-of-the-art computer software reasonably well for two to three years. The prices of desktop computers have remained constant since 1980: about $2000 to $3000, if you shop around. However, your $2000 to $3000 buys more powerful equipment with each passing year.

For example, in 1995 a cost-effective computer is a 486 or Pentium, at least 50 MHz with 8 to 16 MB of RAM and a 300 MB hard disk drive, an SVGA color monitor, and MS-DOS. Figure 5 (page 36) gives complete specifications for this configuration.

Optional Equipment

Figure 6 (page 37) lists items that will add $300 to $400 to your cost. Wait to buy them until you need them. For the foreseeable future, computer hardware will become both cheaper and better as time goes by.

Figure 5.
A Cost-Effective Desktop
Computer System

- 486 or Pentium microprocessor, at least 50 MHz. Don't get an SX computer because the small difference in price is not worth the loss in performance. Look for the term "DX" or "DX" instead.
- A full-size computer case desktop or tower case with a 250-watt power supply.
- 300 MB IDE hard disk drive, 500 MB is better. Buy two hard drives if you can afford it. You can use one hard drive as a method to back up critical files on the other.
- 5¼" high-density floppy drive.
- 3½" high-density floppy drive.
- A tape drive.
- At least one more empty drive bay to add a CD-ROM or tape drive now or later.
- 8 to 16 MB of RAM, 32 to 64 MB total RAM capacity.
- 128 KB to 256 KB memory cache.
- At least 6 slots; 8 is better.
- Two serial ports. Make sure one of the serial ports is high speed.
- One parallel port.
- 101-key extended keyboard.
- Mouse. A dedicated mouse port will leave your serial ports free for other devices.
- SVGA noninterlaced color monitor and a graphics card with at least 1 MB of RAM, 2 MB is better. This combination should permit a display with .28 ms dot pitch (the smaller the pitch, the better the monitor), 16-color 1024x768 resolution (the larger the resolution, the better the monitor), and a 72 Hz horizontal refresh rate.
- A power strip with a surge protector.
- A box of 5¼" floppies and a box of 3½" floppies

Street Price and List Price

Companies advertise both hardware and software at **list price,** which is full retail. If you shop around, you can buy these products at a lower **street** (discount) **price.**

Figure 6. Optional Items

- 14.4 BPS V.32 and V.42 bis internal or external fax modem to access online services such as Westlaw or LEXIS.
- Double-spin internal or external CD-ROM drive.
- A personal label printer (PLP) for printing nice-looking labels on thermal label paper. Your laser printer can also print labels, but you've to change the paper to do it. A laser printer is handy for printing many labels at once, whereas a PLP is handy for occasional label printing.

Printers

Printer costs vary widely. For example:
- $300 for a low-end ink-jet printer like the Hewlett-Packard (HP) DeskJet 500, which has one paper tray, runs at 4 pages per minute (PPM), and has a resolution of 300 dots per inch (dpi);
- $800 for an HP LaserJet 4L (one paper tray, 4 PPM, 300 dpi);
- $1000 for an HP LaserJet 4P (one paper tray, 4 PPM, 600 dpi);
- $1500 for an HP LaserJet IV (one paper tray, 8 PPM, 600 dpi);
- $3000 for an HP LaserJet IVSI (17 PPM).

The quality of the printout from ink-jet printers is acceptable for all law-office documents, but laser printer quality is better. If you print a lot—if you're an appellate lawyer, for example—buy the best laser printer you can afford.

Portable Computers

Cost-effective portable computers are about one generation behind desktop computers. In mid-1994, this means a 386 or 486 microprocessor and a black-and-white screen. Soon, cost-effective portable computers will have a 486 microprocessor and a color screen.

Future Configurations

To learn about the latest computer equipment, go to a computer store or a bookstore with a computer section. Look among the plethora of computer trade magazines for a cover that includes the words "BEST NEW COMPUTERS FOR 199x!" or the equivalent.

Intel hopes that its new processor chip, the Pentium, will be the chip of choice for computer manufacturers. However, Pentium computers may face stiff competition from the Power PCs based on the new Motorola Power PC chip. The Motorola chip promises to be cheaper and run faster and cooler than the Pentium chip.

Both IBM and Apple make Power PCs. Other computer manufacturers are able to use the Motorola chip, too. Power PCs can run several different operating systems. The Power PC will do well if consumers find its benefits readily apparent and current software runs on it seamlessly.

Saving Money

You'll save a few hundred dollars by buying equipment one generation behind the most cost-effective equipment. In mid-1994, this means a computer with a 386 processor instead of a 486 or Pentium processor. The 386 computers can run DOS-based programs well, but if you want to run Windows-based programs, buy a 486 or Pentium computer.

- Avoid computers two or more generations behind. In mid-1994, this means computers with 80286 or 8086 processors. The bang-for-the-dollar ratio for these computers is poor. Unless the computer costs about one tenth (or less) of state-of-the-art computers, the vendor is trying to recoup his or her investment in the equipment at your expense.
- Color monitors run about $300. You can save about $200 if you buy a **monochrome** (black-and-white) **monitor,** but you'll lose the advantages of a color monitor. For example:
  - The Word for Windows document comparison feature makes revisions easier to spot because they're marked in blue.
  - Composing is easier when you can put unedited text in green and edited text in black.
  - Finding urgent items in your electronic calendar or your electronic to-do list is easier when you highlight these items in magenta.
  - Identifying nonpaying clients is easier when you mark their names in red.

You can save about $100 if you buy a computer with one small hard disk or only one floppy drive or less than 4 MB of RAM, but you'll lose productivity and patience every time you stare at your screen while your computer grinds away at its task. However, you can easily upgrade these components later: you can buy a second bigger hard disk, a second floppy drive, or more RAM.

You may save $50 to $100 by buying a cheap keyboard or mouse, but don't scrimp on devices like these that you'll use continually. Cheap keyboards and mice break easily and are hard to use.

Avoid buying used equipment unless you know what you're doing. For example, a small law firm recently bought a PC XT for $1000. The XT is a ten-year-old computer worth $200 at most, worth nothing if its buyer wants to run today's software. The lawyers were stuck with less than one twentieth of the power of a new computer at about one half to one third of the cost. They can create documents with the XT, but the computer will be costly to repair, replacement parts will be hard to get, and the warranty expired a long time ago.

Splurging

Buy the best color monitor you can afford. It will be easy on your eyes and make computing a pleasure. If you have $700–$900 to spare, buy a 17″ Viewsonic with the highest resolution and pixel count you can get. If you have $900 to spare, buy a pivoting 15″ color monitor so you can view the screen in both portrait (8½″ by 11″) and landscape (11″ by 8½″) modes. With a pivoting monitor in portrait position, you can view a whole page of text on the screen at once. (Portrait Display Labs makes pivoting monitors.)

Buy the biggest hard disk you can afford. You'll run out of hard disk space sooner than you think.

Sources

Mail-order houses such as Gateway 2000 in South Dakota (800-GATE-WAY) have good deals on reliable computers and computer support. However, some mail-order customers have suffered significant delays in computer delivery and repairs. Ask the mail-order vendor what delays may occur.

Leasing lets you get a computer without paying a lot of money up front. At this writing you can lease a Gateway 486 DX, 66 MHz computer for $99 a month with a two-year lease.

Local independent dealers assemble and sell DOS-compatibles. Take a computer-savvy friend with you when you talk to these dealers.

Discount computer retail stores such as CompUSA are good sources for modems, printers, floppy disks, software, notebook computers, and—sometimes—desktop computers.

Mail-order catalogs are a good way to browse for computers, peripherals, software, books, and miscellaneous equipment (e.g., floppy disks, dust covers, laser-jet toner, boards, cables). Below is a partial list, in alphabetical order. Most of these catalogs are from independent dealers; the few that come from manufacturers of computer products are noted.

Hardware and Software Catalogs

- Comark (800/955-1481)
- CompuAdd Express (800/925-3000)
- CompUSA (800/COMPUSA)
- Computer Discount Warehouse (800/449-4CDW)
- Crazy Bob's (800/776-5865)
- Dak (800/DAK-0800)
- Elektek (800/395-1000; in Illinois 708/677-7660)
- Global Software and Hardware (800/8-GLOBAL)
- Insight (800/488-0005)
- MicroWarehouse (800/367-7080)
- PC Connection (800/800-5555)
- Z Direct (800/CARE360) (from Zenith Data Systems)

Software Catalogs for the Mass-Market

- Egghead Software (800/EGGHEAD)
- Public Brand Software (800/426-3475)
- Shareware Express (800/346-2842)
- Surplus Software (800/753-7877)
- Tiger Software (800/88-TIGER)
- The PC Zone (800/258-2088)

Miscellaneous Catalogs

- Computer Supplies Digest (800/544-3472)
- Damark (800/729-9000)
- Data-Cal Computer Productivity Enhancements (800/223-0123)
- Deluxe Legal Forms and Stationery (800/336-4171)
- Inmac (800/547-5444)
- Global Computer Supplies (800/8-GLOBAL)
- Lyben Computer Systems (8108-8100)
- OfficeMax (800/788-8080)
- Power Up! Direct (800/851-2917)

- BlackBox Catalog (412/746-5530; toll-free Fax 800/321-0746)
- Jameco Electronic Components (800/831-4242)

Books

- CompuBooks (800/880-6818)
- Sybex Report (800/227-2346) (from Sybex, Inc.)

Product Lists for the Legal Market

- ABA LPM Publishing provides excellent product and user information. Call 312/988-5522 for a catalog, or see page 139.
- The ABA Technology Clearinghouse has packets of information, available for a nominal fee, on legal-market applications. Call 312/988-5465 for a catalog.

Precautions

When you buy computer equipment, check the manuals that come with the equipment first, if possible. The manuals should explain how to set up the equipment and include illustrations.

Buy computer equipment from a company with a 30-day return policy. After you buy the equipment, check it out right away.

Most computer stores and mail-order houses have a one-year warranty on parts and service for computers and computer devices. If they don't, go somewhere else.

Question. A computer guru who should know better bought a $550 SCSI hard drive from a discount mail-order house in California. The vendor required payment by cashier's check before delivery. The SCSI drive was temperamental. The guru decided to return it but couldn't. What did this guru do wrong?

Answer. The guru should have shopped elsewhere. He did save $100 on his purchase but lost the privilege of disputing it via the credit card company. The discount house promised satisfaction but went out of business two weeks later.

Find out how the store or mail-order house implements the warranty. Does the warranty include on-site repairs? Can you take malfunctioning equipment to the store for repair? Count on losing at least a day or two if you do. Must you ship the equipment back to the manufacturer for repair? Count on losing a week or more of computer use.

If you order a computer from a mail-order house, you can't test it out

A Pop Quiz

Question. *What if I want to add to the computer I have now—to buy a CD-ROM drive, for example. How do I go about it?*

Caution. Before you go shopping, make sure you know what kind of computer you've. Is it a Macintosh or a PC? A 286, 386, 486, or Pentium PC? Do you've room for a internal or external CD-ROM drive on your machine? Review the material on peripherals in chapter 3 if you're not sure.

Short answer. Browse a computer store or a catalog for CD-ROM drives. Look at the price range. What's the lowest priced drive? The highest price drive? Pick something in the middle with a brand name you recognize. Make sure it comes with a warranty and that you can return it.

Long answer. Go to a computer store or look at one of the catalogs you sent away for. Find the section on CD-ROM drives. Make a table of CD-ROM drives available. Include brand name, price, size, and speed in the table. Remember that for CD-ROMs, both access time and transfer rate are important speed measurements.

If you have accumulated trade magazines for the past few months or so, look in your collection for a recent article on CD-ROM drives. Otherwise, go to your nearest large library and look up the same thing. What seems to be the current "best bang for the buck" drive—the best specifications for the least money? In mid-1994 it's a double or triple speed SCSI drive selling for $200 to $300.

before you buy it, so make sure you can send it back. *Deal only with companies that will let you pay with a credit card.*

Misleading Specifications

Beware of quotations for computer configurations in the following circumstances:

- The price looks great, but a crucial component is missing, such as the monitor, a hard disk, or the keyboard. (The ad might specify "monitor and keyboard extra" in fine print.)
- The price looks great, but critical specifications are missing, such as the resolution of the monitor or the amount of RAM.
- The price looks great, but key components such as the monitor, hard disk, keyboard, or mouse are substandard.
- The price looks great because the configuration includes equipment not normally bundled with a computer, such as a printer, a CD-ROM, or a modem. This equipment may be obsolete, inferior, or both.

Misleading Advertisements

The examples below demonstrate how technical terms are sometimes finessed in advertisements.

- An advertisement for a hard disk claims that the disk "holds up to 160 MB" of information. It cannot. This disk has a true capacity of 80 MB. This claim rests on the assumption that you can compress up to 160 MB of information into an 80 MB space.
- Hard disk drive manufacturers often specify hard disk sizes using 1,000,000-byte megabytes instead of the full-sized 1,048,576-byte megabytes.
- An advertisement for a Windows product claimed the product could handle "long file names," implying strongly but incorrectly that the product's designers had overcome the DOS file name length limitation (discussed in chapter 5). They had not.

Buyer's Remorse

Just after you purchase your computer, better, faster machines will come on the market. Some lawyers believe they should wait to purchase until that expensive computer everyone raves about comes down in price. When it does, an even better-looking expensive computer will come on the market. Buy the most cost-effective computer available now, set it up, learn how to use it, and go back to practicing law full-time.

Chapter 5

Computer Traffic

T hink of the operating system as the computer's traffic controller and electronic files as the computer's traffic. Everything you do with computer software—including evaluating, buying, and using software— will require a basic understanding of operating systems and files.

Computer Traffic
- Operating systems
  - User interfaces
  - Windows vs. DOS
- Files
  - Names
  - Directories
  - Organization
  - Formats
- Utility software

Operating Systems

The operating system is computer software that controls the computer's flow of information. Every PC or Macintosh computer you buy will come with an operating system. All other software you buy for your computer should be able to run on that operating system.

Right now operating systems are hot topics in the computer world. Most desktop computers nowadays are IBM-compatible computers running **MS-DOS,** an operating system manufactured by Microsoft. MS-DOS is ill-equipped to handle current "multimedia" devices and software. However, none of the heavily advertised operating systems poised to replace MS-DOS, such as IBM's OS/2 and Microsoft Windows NT, is ready for the mainstream computer marketplace. For what these new operating systems give you, they are too difficult to install and use.

A new version of Microsoft Windows, still under development, promises to combine MS-DOS with Microsoft Windows to produce an operating system with a GUI interface. If it does everything the trade press says it will and if it is backward-compatible, it will become the industry standard for PCs.

Operating System User Interfaces

When you turn on a computer and look at its screen, you're looking at the operating system's **user interface.** When you give commands to a computer, you're giving them to the computer through the operating system's user interface. (All other programs, such as word processors and spreadsheets, have user interfaces, too.)

MS-DOS has a command-line user interface, meaning that users must give all instructions to the computer by typing commands on the keyboard. Some operating systems on the market, such as OS/2, Windows NT, and NextStep by NeXT Computer, Inc., have a graphical user interface (GUI).

Microsoft Windows

Microsoft Windows, first mentioned in chapter 2, is not an operating system. Instead, it's one way to make MS-DOS look like an operating system with a GUI. (To confuse things, people often refer to Windows as an operating *environment.*)

To run Microsoft Windows, you type in the command WIN at the MS-DOS command line. Figure 7 shows an example of what first appears on your screen when you run Windows.

Once you're "in Windows," you can use Windows programs such as word processors and spreadsheets. Following are a few advantages of using Windows programs instead of DOS programs.

- A **graphical user interface** (GUI) such as Windows eliminates the need to enter computer commands in a precise and tedious-to-learn form. Instead of typing a computer command, you use the **mouse** (a pointing device) to select **icons,** pictorial representations of computer commands, and to point to a list of command choices on a **menu.**
- Unlike most DOS applications, GUI programs show you on screen exactly how your document will look when you print it. This is called **WYSIWYG** (What You See Is What You Get), pronounced "wizzy wig."
- Most DOS programs display only 25 lines of up to 80 characters each on the screen. GUI programs can display much more text on a screen, and the text looks nicer and is easier to read.
- Windows makes it convenient to run more than one computer program at a time on a PC. For example, users of a word processor can switch to using a **personal information manager** (software that handles miscellaneous bits of information well) without exiting from the word processing program.

Figure 7: The Windows Program Manager

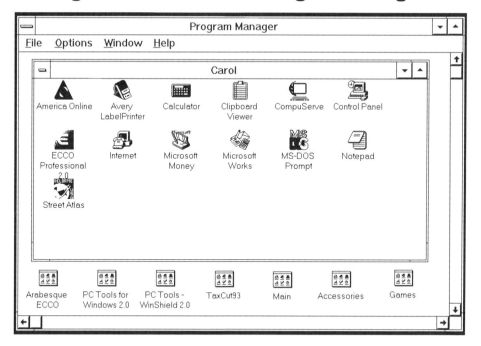

- Windows also makes it convenient to **cut and paste**—to transfer information within programs and from one program to another using the **clipboard.** For example, you can copy your settlement calculations from a spreadsheet into a clipboard. Then you can paste (insert) these calculations from the clipboard into a document in your word processor.

- To some extent, Microsoft Windows has brought standardization of commands and easier-to-use software to the PC world. Menus and help screens in Windows programs are in the same format. **Help screens** display text on screen that should help you when you're stuck. Unlike DOS-based applications, with Windows you need set up your printer only one time, and it will work with all your Windows applications.

- Once you purchase and learn a Windows-based product, you'll find other Windows-based products easier to use. However, although most Windows-based applications do look similar, programs from different publishers perform the same functions differently.

DOS Applications

Following are a few advantages of using DOS-based applications:
- You can get away with buying older less expensive computer hardware.

Figure 8: The Windows File Manager

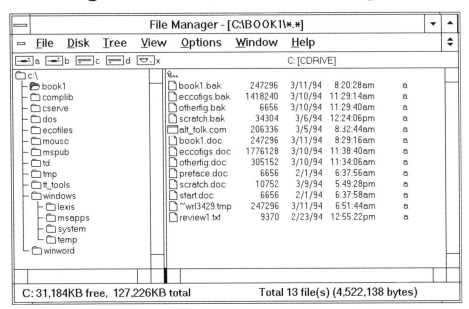

- Many veteran computer users still prefer DOS-based applications.
- DOS applications run faster than GUI applications.
- When you run only DOS applications, there's one less layer of software to cause trouble.

Files

A **file** is the computer's basic unit of information. A file can contain electronic information such as a letter, a brief, or a table listing your cases. These files are often called data files or just **data.** Alternately, a file can contain instructions that direct the computer to do a certain task, such as word processing. These **executable** files are often called *executables,* the *computer program,* the *program,* the *application,* or the *software.*

File Names

Every file has a name to identify it to the computer. How files are named depends on the operating system you're using. In MS-DOS, the length of **file names** is limited to 11 characters (bytes). (The limitations on file name length and conventional memory size are what MS-DOS users complain about most.)

In most operating systems, the name of a file will tell you whether the file is a data file or an executable file. Executable files enable you to create data files. For example, word processing computer software includes an executable file that you run to create a document such as a letter or a brief. Time/billing computer software includes an executable file that you run to keep track of your time and send out bills.

File Directories

Most operating systems organize files in a hierarchical structure. MS-DOS uses a *directory structure*. Each MS-DOS directory is a collection of files. Each directory also may have directories under it, called *subdirectories*. Using directories, you can classify files logically: for example, client Brown's files in one directory, client Smith's files in another, and the files that run your word processing program in a third.

Figure 8 shows a list of directories and files in Microsoft Windows.

The highest-level directory in your computer is called the **root directory.** The root directory should contain subdirectories for computer programs and other subdirectories for client files. Each of these subdirectories can have subdirectories of their own.

Organizing your files

Keep client and other document files in directories separate from your program directories—for example, don't put a client's deposition transcript in the same directory as WordPerfect. Files that belong together, such as all of the documents for a single client, should go in the same subdirectory.

Question. A local prosecutor's office automated several years ago. The word processing was delegated to one secretary who recently retired. The lawyers in the office were unable to find the documents they needed after the secretary left. Why?

Answer. This secretary had put all documents in the root directory, not in subdirectories whose names might have given others a clue to the documents' contents. All the documents had short cryptic DOS file names, and the secretary had not used the feature available in most word processors that would have allowed him to identify each document more fully.

File Formats

Computer programs create files in particular file formats. For example, WordPerfect is a word processor and the files it creates are in WordPerfect format. File formats are either standard or proprietary.

Specifications for creating **standard file formats** are public. For example, Microsoft Word, another word processor, cannot read files in WordPerfect format directly. However, because Word knows how to read and write WordPerfect files, Word can convert word processing files from WordPerfect to Word format, and vice versa.

With **proprietary file formats,** only the vendor that created the file knows how to read and write files in that format. You'll find it difficult to use and convert files in proprietary formats without consulting the vendor first. Programs written for the legal market often use proprietary file formats and don't include a way to convert these files to standard file format.

Once electronic information is in a file, you should never have to reenter it again. However, it's harder to reuse information in proprietary formats than that in standard formats. Try to buy programs that keep your files in standard formats, so you can use them with other programs conveniently.

Make sure you know what file format you're working with.

Also make sure you know what kind of computer created the file you want to use.

Utility Software

All operating systems provide commands that let you manipulate files—to copy, move, delete, or rename them. **Utility programs** supplement operating system commands. These programs (1) do what operating system commands do, only better; (2) do what operating systems commands should do, but don't; or (3) enable hardware devices to work with your computer. Table 7 gives examples of utility software, including functions and brand names you may have heard of.

Question. *A lawyer wanted to change the* **autoexec.bat** *and* **config.sys** *files that tell the computer what to do when it starts up. He ran WordPerfect on these files to make these changes. When he rebooted his computer (started it up again), the computer would not work. Why?*

Answer. Because the autoexec.bat and config.sys files must be in **ASCII format**, a standard file format that any PC can read. The lawyer had saved the files in WordPerfect format, which the computer couldn't read when it started up. If the lawyer had used the WordPerfect program to save the files in ASCII format, the computer could have read them when it rebooted.

Hint: You should always keep a copy of your most recent autoexec.bat and config.sys files on a floppy disk. See Appendix A for more information on backing up.

Analogy to the Real World

Analogies are tricky, because ideas don't always map well from the computer world to the real world. Table 8 (page 52) is a (slightly tongue-in-cheek) table of the concepts in this chapter and the closest real world analogy.

Give the same thought to organizing your electronic files that you give to your paper files. You

Question. A lawyer colleague gives you a file on a floppy disk. She created the file on her Macintosh computer. You insert the disk into the floppy drive of your PC and try to list its files with the Windows file manager. The computer says it cannot read the floppy disk. What does this mean?

Answer. PCs cannot read floppy disks created by Macintosh computers. Therefore, the Windows file manager cannot list or read the files on the disk. However, conversion software such as "Software Bridge" lets you convert Macintosh files to a format that a PC can read.

Table 7: Utility Software

Type of utility	Function	Brand Names (a noninclusive list)
Compression software	Compresses files so they take up less space on your hard disk	PKZIP
Synchronization software	Keeps the files of your portable computer in sync with the files of your desktop computer	LapLink
File viewing	Views the contents of your files, no matter what format they're in	Central Point PC Tools for Windows
File management	Lists and manipulates directory and file names	Windows File Manager Central Point PC Tools for Windows Norton Desktop for Windows
File searching	Looks for "lost" files by searching on file names; looks for words and phrases in one or more files	Central Point PC Tools for Windows
Virus checking	Checks for computer viruses (see Appendix A for details on virus software)	DOS includes one; so does Central Point PC Tools for Windows and Norton Desktop for Windows
Communications	Enables a modem to work	Windows Terminal, ProComm, SmartComm
Scanning	Enables an optional scanner to work	Omnipage
Voice recognition	Enables a voice recognition device to work	DragonDictate

would not throw all your client paper files in one folder, and you should not throw all your client electronic files in one directory either.

Table 8: Computer Analogy to the Real World	
Computer Term	Real World Analogy
Operating system	Your office manager
Operating system user Interface	Your office manager's personality
Byte	Typed character
File	A document such as a letter or a brief
Directory	A file folder
A hard disk	A file drawer
All the permanent storage in your computer	A file cabinet
File formats	(Very roughly!) If you have a file cabinet with 8.5" by 11" file drawers, you'll have a tough time stuffing 8.5" by 14" pages in them
Utilities	File clerks and muscular people who move office furniture
A network	Lots of file cabinets, all talking to each other in voices you cannot hear

Chapter 6

How Computer Applications Work

The previous chapter discussed operating system and utility software. This chapter discusses the computer applications you'll use most in your law practice—the programs that let you tell the computer what to do with the contents of files. For example, a word processing application program lets you handle electronic documents, such as a letter or a brief. A time/billing application lets you handle electronic time and expense records.

When you understand this material on computer applications, you'll understand what a computer can do for you and what it can't. You'll have a good start on being able to see if you really need the programs vendors want to sell you.

How Computer Applications Work
- Contents of a computer file
- Text
  - Word processing
  - Search and retrieval
- Images
  - Graphics
  - Desktop publishing
  - Presentations
  - Optical character recognition
- Sounds
- Tables
  - Word processing
  - Spreadsheets
  - Databases

What's in a Computer File?

Think of the electronic information in computer data files as being organized as follows:

- Text—words strung together
- Images—pictures either drawn on the computer or optically scanned into the computer
- Sounds—audio recordings made by the computer or a human
- Tables—for example, a list of cases you otherwise would keep on a yellow pad or the record of checks you otherwise would keep in a paper check register

A single computer data file can contain one or more of these forms of information. This chapter describes these forms of information in detail and the computer functions that apply to them. This chapter also introduces the computer applications that operate on each of these forms.

Mass-market computer applications are aimed toward a wide range of computer users. Mass-market applications include word processors, search and retrieval programs, desktop publishing, optical character recognition (OCR), voice recognition, spreadsheets and database programs. **Legal-market** applications are aimed toward lawyers and law offices. Legal-market applications include back office applications, such as time/billing, and substantive applications, such as wills and trusts software.

Text

A letter to your client is text. So is a contract, a brief, a memo, a note you send by electronic mail, and the transcript of a deposition spanning several weeks. Cases you **download** (retrieve) from Westlaw and LEXIS are text.

With a computer, you can perform editing and searching functions on text. Editing text means entering, adding, changing, and deleting all or parts of it. Searching text means looking for words and phrases in it.

Word Processors

Word processing software lets you edit text files. For example, if you used *implied* when you meant *inferred* in a letter to your client, you can use a word processor to fix your mistake. You can move text around to reorganize your document. You can write an angry letter and then edit it into a civilized form. You can apply underlining, boldface, and different type fonts to your text.

Word processing programs can do simple word searches on one or more text files. For example, you could find, one at a time, all the occurrences of "asbestos" or "slip and fall" in an electronic file of your colleague's brief. Unless you deal with huge litigation documents routinely, this simple search capability will be adequate for your needs. Word processors will choke on very large text files such as monster depositions.

Search and Retrieval Software

In litigation you often need to search for words and phrases in discovery documents. Search and retrieval programs let you do these searches, often called *full-text searches*, quickly. With search and retrieval programs, you can perform complex searches for combinations of text in one or more files and display all the hits (the paragraphs where the text appears) at once. For example, you can find all occurrences of "asbestos" that appear in the same paragraph with "construction worker." You can use **pattern matching** to find text. For example, with a search for "sm*", you can find all occurrences of words beginning with "sm." (The asterisk in "sm*" is called a **wildcard character.** There are many kinds of wildcard characters. However, if you remember the asterisk, you will know about 90% of what you need to know to perform most of searches you'll need to do.)

Unlike word processing programs, search and retrieval programs do fast searches. Word processing searches are slow because they search through every word in the text file(s) to see if it matches the search query. Search and retrieval programs do indexed searching, meaning they

- copy every word from every text file into a separate file, called an index.
- sort the entries in the index alphabetically. The content of an index file looks something like a concordance.
- search the index, not the full text, for the word or phrase you want. These searches go quickly, for the same reason that you can more easily find a name in your Rolodex because the cards are in alphabetical order rather than strewn all over your desk.

Images

An image is a picture. The photograph of a computer in figure 3 of this book is an image. Windows word processors let you insert images into your word processing documents. Image files typically are large,

Figure 9: Scanned Image

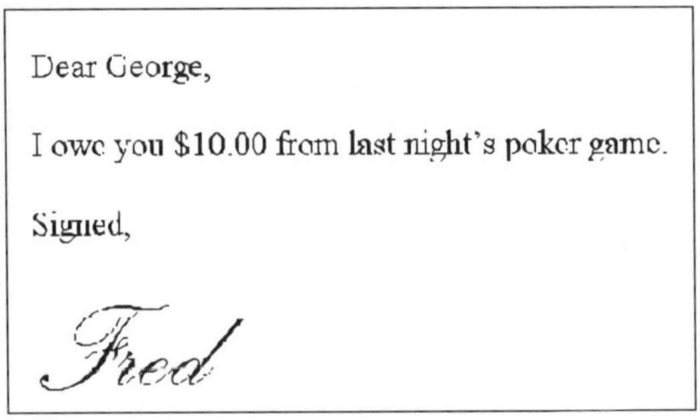

Dear George,

I owe you $10.00 from last night's poker game.

Signed,

Fred

Figure 10: Edited Image

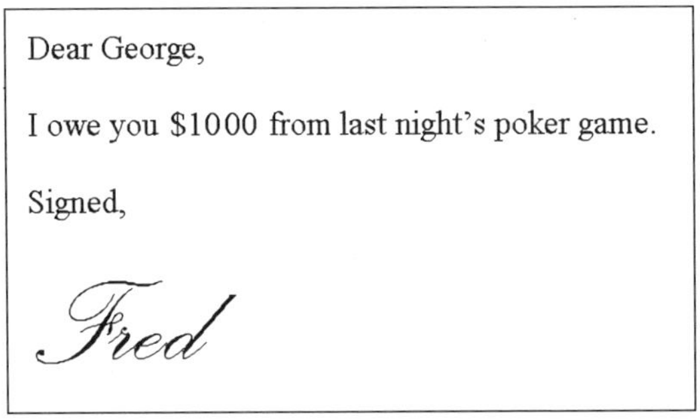

Dear George,

I owe you $1000 from last night's poker game.

Signed,

Fred

compared to text files. For example, the illustrations for this book took 2 MB of storage.

Graphics Software

You can edit images with a **graphics program.** The image in figure 9 is a hypothetical paper contract scanned into the computer with an optical scanner.

Figure 10 shows the scanned image after it was edited with Paintbrush, a graphics program that comes with Microsoft Windows.

You can buy more expensive graphics editing software for the PC, including programs that can edit photographs flawlessly.

Desktop Publishing Software

With desktop publishing (DTP) software, you can incorporate several text and image files into a single file, where you can arrange the text and images any way you want. Then you can print the file yourself on a high-resolution printer or send the file to a printing service. (Be warned that DTP programs usually cannot read files created by different DTP programs.)

Presentation Programs

Presentation software enables you to incorporate text and image files into a file that can be used for overhead projections. (Presentation programs usually cannot read files created by different presentation programs.)

Optical Character Recognition

An optical scanner can take a picture of a printed page, such as a contract or a deed. The picture becomes an electronic image in the computer's storage. **Optical character recognition,** or **OCR,** software reads this image and uses image pattern-recognition techniques to convert the image into text. You can then edit this text in your word processor.

OCR software can make mistakes. It works best with clean pages. For example, if a contract is a copy of a copy, it won't scan well. In the past five years OCR techniques have improved enormously and OCR software now includes spelling and other error checking. However, even with a 1% error rate, which is good, a scanned document will have a few mistakes per page.

Question. A lawyer received a fax on her fax modem. She tried to read the fax file with her word processor but couldn't. Why?

Answer. The fax file is a type of image file. Word processors cannot read fax files directly. However, fax modem programs often have OCR capabilities. The lawyer can use the OCR feature in her fax program to convert her fax file into a text file that her word processor can read.

Sounds

With a microphone and a hardware device called a **sound board,** you can make voice recordings on your computer and play them back with Windows software. For example, with Word for Windows, a word processor, you can make voice-recorded annotations to documents. (When you review a colleague's document this way, you can truly speak your mind.)

Like image files, sound files can easily take up inordinate amounts of room on your hard disk.

Voice Recognition

A **voice recognition** hardware device can record a human voice. Voice recognition software converts these sounds into instructions a computer can recognize. These instructions can be commands to the computer or text in a word processing document. Like OCR software, voice recognition devices can make mistakes.

In the past year or two voice recognition has improved enormously, but with many voice recognition devices, it's still cumbersome to talk to a computer because every word must be separated by a brief pause.

Tables

Finally, electronic information can be in table form. Tables are a way of organizing information so that you can treat like types of information in like ways. For example, your checkbook register is a table. You treat the deposit, withdrawal, and balance columns in this table as numbers on which you can perform arithmetic operations. You treat the payee name and memo column as text. You treat the payment date column as a date.

Word Processing Software

Most word processors can organize information in tables, sort it, and do simple arithmetic on it. The tables in this book were created in a word processor. Word processors enable you to incorporate tables generated by a spreadsheet or database program. For example, you can include a spreadsheet table (see below) of settlement negotiations in a letter to a client.

Spreadsheet Software

Spreadsheet programs work on tables of numbers. For example, with a spreadsheet you can easily calculate payments at 10% interest and then recalculate them at 15% interest. Figure 11 shows calculations at 10% interest.

In figure 12, the 10% interest amount in cell B2 (that is, Row B, column 2) has been changed (edited) to 15%.

Underlying Cell B3, the amount due at end of year, is a user-created formula telling the spreadsheet to multiply cell B1 by cell B2 and display the result. (The formula will look something like this: =B1*B2). When you change the contents of cell B2, the result in cell B3 changes automatically.

Database Software

With a database program, computers can work with the electronic equivalent of, for example, a table of cases on a yellow pad. Most applications

Figure 11: Calculations at 10% Interest Rate

Row # /Column #	Column 1	Column 2	Column 3
Row A	Amount loaned	Simple Interest for one year	Amount due at end of year
Row B	$100,000	10%	$110,000

Figure 12: Changed to 15% Interest Rate

Row # /Column #	Column 1	Column 2	Column 3
Row A	Amount loaned	Simple Interest for one year	Amount due at end of year
Row B	$100,000	15%	$115,000

designed especially for law offices are written using database programs. The next chapter goes into databases and database applications in detail.

Summary

Table 9 (page 60) summarizes the information in this section.

Table 9: Summary of Forms of Information

Form of Information	Applications That Work on Them	Examples of What You Can Do with These Applications	Markets Written for	Brand Names (a Noninclusive List)
Text	Word processors	Create letters, memos, briefs	Mass	WordPerfect
	Search and retrieval programs	Search depositions and transcripts	Mass	Zyindex
	Hypertext	Set up a law firm research database	Mass	Folio Views
Images	Word processors	Add a logo to your laser-printed letterhead	Mass	Microsoft Word
	Desktop publishing programs	Add eye-catching graphics to your client newsletter	Mass	Quark
	Presentation programs	Create slide shows	Mass	Lotus Freelance Graphics
	Optical character recognition	Convert a paper copy of a lease or contract into text	Mass	Caere Omnipage
	Graphics programs	Create pictures; touch up photographs	Mass	Adobe Illustrator
Sounds	Word processors	Add voice-generated annotations to word processing documents	Mass	Lotus AmiPro
	Voice recognition	Dictate to your computer	Mass	DragonDictate
	Music	Compose music	Mass	ConcertWare
Tables	Word processors	Add a simple table of expenses to a letter	Mass	WordPerfect
	Spreadsheets	Determine the consequences of refinancing your mortgage	Mass	Borland Quattro Pro
	Database applications	Design your own law-firm database; do your taxes and accounting; run a bankruptcy practice; keep a marketing database (See the next chapter.)	Mass and legal	Borland Paradox Lotus Approach Microsoft Access

Chapter 7

What You Need to Know About Databases

A database program works on information in table form. When you hear that you can do much more with your computer than word processing, that "much more" frequently means using database applications. Databases let you store more information than in

> **What You Need to Know About Databases**
> - What a database is
> - What you can do with a database
> - Database applications
>   - Generic programs
>   - Specialized programs
>   - Personal information managers
>   - Legal-market applications

the precomputer age and analyze that information more thoroughly. When a lawyer or other legal professional is known as a "power user," it means he or she uses database technology effectively.

What Is a Database?

Suppose you create a table of all of your cases on a yellow pad. Each line in the table represents one case and includes the case name, client name, responsible lawyer, and a few notes. You can do little with this information on the yellow pad. You can erase or scratch stuff out, but that gets messy. Once the table gets big, it's difficult to find what you need in it.

Once you put this case information into a computer, you can edit your information easily. You can sort your entries by case name, client name, or responsible lawyer. You can locate all clients with the word "urgent" in their notes. With a computer, it becomes practical to keep more information about each client, such as birthdays and more extensive notes.

When you enter a client's information into a computer, each case

Case Table

Case Number	Case Name	Client Name	Responsible Lawyer	Other Case Information
1	Alpha v. Beta	ABC Insurance	CMW	
2	In re Gamma	DEF Mutual	DJD	
3	Delta Real Estate Matter	ABC Insurance	CMW	

Docket Table

Case Number	Docket Event	Other Docket Information
1	Motion	
1	Meeting with client	
2	Trial date	

Time/billing Table

Case Number	Time and Expense Transaction	Other Time and Expense Information
1	Telephone call	
3	Prepare memo	

becomes a row in a table kept by the computer. The information for each case becomes columns in the table. The table itself is the database.

More sophisticated database applications work on several tables of electronic information at once. For example, above are tables of insurance defense cases and related information.

You might have other tables related to your case table. For example, you could have a table of docket events for your cases and a table of time and expense transactions for your cases.

In computerese, a collection of one or more tables is a database, the rows in the table are records, and the columns in the table are fields. Computer applications that work on databases are **database programs.**

Database programs that can handle only one table at a time are **flat-file database** programs. Database programs that can collect and report on information on more than one table are **relational database** programs. (The complete "computer science" definition of relational databases is much more complex than this.)

Information in tables is usually in text form. Depending on the software, however, tables also can include images and sounds.

What Can You Do with a Database?

Database applications let you manipulate information in tables using the following functions:

- **Edit.** Database programs let you edit tables such as the ones above. For example, you could change "Prepare memo" in the time/billing table above to "Prepare motion."
- **Search.** In the case table above, suppose you wanted to locate information for a case, and you remembered the case name began with "Alpha." You could search the case name field for "Alpha."
- **Sort.** You can sort any of the columns on a table. For example, you could sort the case table above by the date you opened each case.
- **Filter.** This function lets you see those rows of a table that meet the criteria you specify. For example, you could ask the computer to show just the docket events for client Brown.
- **Calculate.** With this function you could, for example, get a total of the hours you've spent on *Brown v. Brown* this month.
- **Merge.** You can merge information from tables into a text file. Suppose you want to send a form letter to your estate planning clients to notify them of a change in the law. You could tell the computer to use the filter function to select your estate planning clients. You could then tell the computer to merge the resulting table with a text file containing your form letter. The result will be "personalized form letters" to your clients.

With database software, you can use these functions on a combination of the above tables because all of these tables have the case numbers in common. In database terminology, the tables are **linked.**

Questions That Database Applications Can Answer

When electronic information is stored in a database—for example, in the set of tables above—then you can use database applications to answer questions such as the ones below.

- "How many cases did we take on last month?" Answering this question requires the case table above, the Filter function to find all the cases that were taken on last month, and the Calculate function to calculate the total number of cases in this group.

- "Where are all the lawyers in the firm today and what cases are they working on?" Answering this question requires the case table above and the Filter function to find today's events, along with each event's case, location, and responsible lawyer.
- "How much work have we done for client Brown this month?" Answering this question requires the time/billing table above, the Filter function to find the month's transactions for client Brown, and the Calculate function to determine how many hours and dollars the firm has racked up on behalf of Brown this month.

Database programs deliver the answers to these questions as reports. Good database programs can display reports on the screen, send them to the printer, or write them to an electronic file for editing later. Database programs perform these operations whether you use a keyboard, scribble on a pen-based computer, or talk to your computer's voice recognition device. As computers become more user-friendly, you'll find it more convenient to ask these questions and get answers.

Expert Systems

Suppose you're faced with the following task: "Print answers to complaints for the 500 personal injury cases we are defending for XYZ Pharmaceuticals. Make sure all the different names and jurisdictions are entered correctly in each complaint. Insert paragraph A if the plaintiff has disease X, insert paragraph B if the plaintiff has disease Y."

Assembling documents to fulfill this request requires the case table above, a large text file with the model answer, a small text file containing paragraph A, and another small text file containing paragraph B. The merge function of the "document assembly" database program inserts information from the case table into the model answer, consults the rules applicable to diseases X and Y, picks the correct paragraph to insert into the model answer, and assembles the final answers.

The rules for inserting text can be far more complex than the example above. Expert systems are document assembly database programs that incorporate the knowledge of legal experts as rules. Some programs let you make up your own rules; for example, a first-year associate can easily access the experience of a firm's top contract lawyer by using the firm's customized computer expert system.

The expert system has the potential to aid in the substantive practice of law. For lawyers, the expert system promises to enhance the process of good lawyering. For nonlawyers, the expert system may make available a "lawyer on a disk." Already a few primitive expert systems allow nonlawyers to write a simple will. Other expert systems will undoubtedly become available to, for example, file for divorce, sell and purchase a home, or write a lease for computer equipment.

Asking These Questions Ought to Be Easier Than It Is

With most modern database programs, you cannot ask questions in a natural language form such as "How many cases did we take on last month?" "What are all the documents involving John Brown?" or "Print answers to 500 personal injury complaints." Instead, you must get the answers to these questions by using the techniques described above, that is by telling the computer which electronic functions to apply to which table(s) in your database. Windows software often makes using these functions easier than DOS software does.

The computer industry is making progress toward implementing natural language queries. Westlaw and LEXIS, online services with law-related databases, now enable you to do natural language searches of cases, law review articles, statutes and other legal materials. Previously, online services limited users to **Boolean searches** such as "Adopt! w/5 Child!" (This expression means "find all words that begin with 'adopt' and that are within five words of all words that begin with 'child.' With online services, the exclamation point is a wildcard character.) With Boolean queries, you get exactly the answer to the question you asked, even if it's not the answer you wanted. With natural language queries, the computer has to guess about what you really want because, unlike Boolean queries, natural language queries are imprecise.

Other artificial intelligence techniques being developed, such as neural nets, promise to make asking questions even easier. Eventually these techniques will be common in off-the-shelf database software.

Database Applications

Database applications work on databases. Some database applications enable you to set up your own databases. With other applications, the tables and reports for the database are customized, that is, they're set up for you already, and all you do is enter information and choose options to get reports.

Most programs written especially for the law office are customized database applications. Examples include time/billing, docket control, bankruptcy, and estate planning. Many mass-market database applications are also suitable for law-office use, including personal information managers (PIMs), programs to do your taxes, and programs to handle your checkbook, because you can easily customize them to perform common law-office automation tasks.

Database Software

Database programs let you set up your own tables and use database functions on them to create reports. You could, for example, use a database program to set up a mailing list of all your clients or an inventory of your office equipment. Database programs are both flexible and powerful, but they require considerable time to learn and use well.

Flat-file database programs are less expensive and easier to use than relational database programs. Flat-file databases include Symantic Q&A and Borland Reflex.

Relational database programs marketed to appeal to nonprogrammers include Microsoft Access, Borland Paradox, Lotus Approach, and dBASE, the grandfather of commercial PC relational databases. (Most database programs recognize dBASE format, a de facto standard format.)

Relational database programs used mostly by legal software vendors to create customized applications—for example, financial, legal-market, and personal information management applications—include Clipper and Advanced Revelation.

Specialized Mass-Market Software

Specialized mass-market programs are usually database programs set up by the vendor for specific office applications, such as bookkeeping, accounting, taxes, and professional time/billing.

Personal Information Managers

Of all the software available to lawyers and other legal professionals, the personal information manager (PIM) shows the greatest potential for "case management"—helping you control a law practice from a desktop computer. A PIM is often easier to learn, less expensive, and more flexible than legal-market software available to do the same basic tasks.

Table 10: PIM Table

Type of Program	Examples of Tables	Examples of Reports	Brand Names (a Noninclusive List)
Contact management	Client names, addresses, phone numbers, contact history, status of telephone calls (e.g., when to make a follow-up call)	Whom do I have to call today?	Act! Maximizer
Calendar	Appointments, things-to-do list	A monthly calendar that looks like the one on your wall	OnTime
Scheduling	Rooms available, people available	All one-hour time slots when the big conference room and all the senior partners are available	Microsoft Schedule +
Project management	Project milestones, start dates, due dates, people responsible	Who should be working on what project right now?	Microsoft Project
Hybrids	Do some of each of the above	Some of each of the above	Commence, ECCO, DayTimer

"Specialized" PIMs

Specialized PIMs are usually database applications adapted for people who must track contacts, events, and projects. Table 10 above lists a few types of specialized PIMs and what they do.

"Flexible" PIMs

Lawyers and other legal professionals must continually juggle miscellaneous snippets of text, including

- "left message" notes;
- advice given;
- appointments and docket events;
- things to do;
- things done;
- notes on meetings;
- text of electronic mail you send and receive to and from your staff, your clients, and your colleagues;
- text of other correspondence;
- ideas, thoughts, observations;
- boilerplate contract clauses;
- abstracts of discovery documents;
- witness lists.

These text snippets cry out to be organized by the computer. Sometimes you need to treat them as text—to enter them as free-form variable length text, edit them, move them around, and search for words or phrases in them. At other times you need to organize these text snippets in table form, to sort and to classify for filtering later.

Neither database programs nor most PIMs handle text snippets well. However, flexible PIMs do. (An example of a flexible PIM is ECCO, by Arabesque Software.) With a flexible PIM you can set up the structure of your information any way you want.

Unlike many database products, with a PIM there is no separation of data and reports: the data is the report, the report is the data. For example, when you request a list of clients from a PIM, you can edit a particular client's data without having to exit the report part of the program to go into the editing part of the program. This feature in PIMs makes for a more convenient but less secure information system, because anyone can change information anywhere.

"Pretty" PIMs

Pretty PIMs provide attractive calendars and address books to enter appointments, contacts, and notes. However, pretty PIMs are limited because they give you no way to perform most database operations on your electronic information. You cannot, for example, ask a pretty PIM for all your trial dates for client Brown in the next month. Lotus Organizer is a fine example of a pretty PIM.

Legal-Market Applications

Database applications written for the legal market are frequently database applications that have been adapted for law-office use; that is, the tables and reports in the database have been set up for you already. Table 11 lists a few typical law-office applications and what they do.

All software, whether mass or legal-market, uses the same forms and functions of electronic information discussed earlier in this chapter. Thus, with mass-market applications you can easily replicate some of the basic functions of legal-market database software. Table 12 (page 70) is a table of law-office applications and mass-market programs that can do some of the same tasks.

Before buying an expensive legal application, see if a mass-market product can do what you need. For example, if you decide that you need an automated Rolodex, you don't have to buy an expensive case management

Table 11: Legal-market Applications

Type of Program	Examples of Tables	Examples of Associated Text for Merging	Examples of Reports	Brand names (a Noninclusive List)
Case management (general)	Clients, matters, docket events, time spent	Retainer letter, other correspondence	All information for one client; all clients with no activity in the last month	Legal Edge
Case management (personal injury)	Same as case management plus, e.g., insurance specials, adjusters	Request for medical records	All insurance specials for client Brown	PINS, Saga
Time/billing	Clients, matters, time/billing transactions (Time/billing programs are usually bundled with an accounting program.)	A bill	Client payments 60 days past due; all activity on a court-appointed estate matter	TimeSlips, TABS, Juris
Docket control	More complete docket events, perhaps clients and matters	A calendar	All court dates coming up in the next month	Abacus, CompuLaw
Conflict of Interest	Names of individuals and entities that could conceivably present a conflict of interest to you in the future		All entities related to client Brown	
Document assembly for estate work	Information for wills	A "will template" and alternate boiler-plate clauses		Flexpractice
Document assembly (general)	Whatever you want	Whatever you want, and you make up the rules for what text goes where		Capsoft
Imaging	Descriptions of images and the images themselves			
Document management	Document names, authors, client/matter assignment, and descriptions		All documents written by Attorney Smith	SoftSolutions, PC DOCS
Online services such as LEXIS and WestLaw	Case names, article titles		All cases decided by Justice Marshall.	
Litigation support	Abstracts. (Many packages also do full-text searching.)		All abstracts containing the word "carcinogen"	Summation

system, because a mass-market contact manager will do nicely. Or, if you need a fast way to search through 10 MB of depositions and transcripts for a few words and phrases, you don't have to buy an expensive litigation

Table 12: Corresponding Legal-market and Mass-market Applications	
Legal-Market Software	Mass-Market Equivalents (for the Basics)
Case management (general)	Contact managers (limited) Flexible PIMs
Docket control, calendaring, scheduling	Calendar software Scheduling software Project management software Flexible PIMs
Conflict of Interest	Flexible PIMs Contact managers Mass-market search and retrieval software
Litigation support	Database applications File utility software Search and retrieval software Flexible PIMs
Imaging	Windows database applications Flexible PIMs
Document management	Word processors Flexible PIMs

support system because a mass-market file utility or search and retrieval program will do the job.

However, legal-market software can do things for you that you cannot easily replicate with mass-market software. For example:

- For time/billing, allows credit for client payments to be split among several lawyers
- For docket control, calculates the dates of docket control events automatically
- For litigation support, keeps all information, indexes, and abstracts for a case in one location.
- For substantive areas, generates documents such as bankruptcy and real estate documents
- For document assembly, incorporates the knowledge of legal experts

A Caveat

A lawyer dropped by the LawTech Center one day. "I have exactly 15 minutes to spare," he said. "Please give me the names of programs that can automate our entire domestic practice. I want the names of several good programs that can handle all our documents, billings, cases, pleadings, discovery, clients, dockets, conflicts of interest, whatever."

This lawyer quite reasonably wanted an integrated legal-market application that would work for him straight out of the box. (Integrated applications are based on the relational databases described in the previous chapter.) An integrated application combines traditionally separate applications such as time/billing, docket control, and case management. Integrated applications are based on a relational database.

Good integrated legal-market applications allow you to enter and edit all client and case information in one (and only one) place. They make it possible to learn just one consistent set of commands. Unfortunately for that lawyer, no family-law integrated applications were available.

For a few practice areas, lawyers can buy integrated applications suited to their practice. These applications are often expensive. For example, some corporate counsel systems cost hundreds of thousands of dollars. Some personal injury systems cost tens of thousands of dollars.

Even expensive integrated applications won't do everything you want. What if you want to track and bill time by the hour with your corporate counsel or personal injury system? Most integrated systems won't let you do that. Instead, you must purchase an additional time/billing package that won't integrate with your current system and won't let you easily transfer information to and from your current system (because the file formats of both systems are usually proprietary).

The truth is, anyone who uses a computer must learn several different computer applications and enter the same information more than once. One solo practitioner who uses legal-market DOS-based software complains that she must enter client information at least three times: (1) in a time/billing program, (2) in a docket control program, and (3) in a word processing program. She also observes that she has had to learn three completely different software packages to automate her practice, each with a fairly steep learning curve.

Mass-market Windows applications, flexible PIMs in particular, show the most promise for alleviating these integration and learning-curve problems. Because all Windows applications run in the same Windows operating environment, they're easier to learn. The potential exists to share information conveniently between these applications, even if they're written by different vendors. Unfortunately, this potential is not well exploited yet.

Chapter 8

Before You Buy

Hundreds of publications—available at newsstands, bookstores, and drugstores in the same section as *Cosmopolitan*, *Modern Bride*, and *Guns and Ammo*—provide product descriptions and reviews of mass-market software. The area of legal-market software is covered in detail by

- *Locate 1993-1994*, edited by Mark S. Halperin and Eric M. Hellmer;
- *The Automated Law Firm*, by Richard Robbins, published by Prentice-Hall;
- For a nominal fee, the ABA Technology Clearinghouse supplies information packets on law-office automation topics, including general automation, time/billing, docket control, and special practice areas. The packets include reference sources, software lists, bibliographies, and reprints of articles from law-office automation literature.

The ABA Law Practice Management Section has several publications on real-life applications of mass-market and legal-market software, including

- *Winning with Computers*, Parts 1 and 2, edited by John C. Tredennick Jr. and James A. Eidelman;
- *From Yellow Pads to Computers*, second edition, edited by Kathryn M. Braeman and Fran Shellenberger.

Journals and newsletters include
- ABA *Law Practice Management* Magazine;

Before You Buy
- Check out the publications
- Evaluate the software
- Legal-market software
- Cost
- Is it user-friendly?
- Will it work for you?
- Custom-designed software

- *Law Office Computing*, issued by James Publishing;
- *Leder's Legal Tech Newsletter;*
- *The Lawyer's PC*, published by Shepard's McGraw-Hill;
- *Network 2d*, the quarterly newsletter of the ABA LPM Computer Division, on automating your law practice;
- *WORD Progress*, the newsletter of the ABA LPM Word Processing Interest Group;
- The ABA *Counselor's Computer & Management Report*, advice on software for corporate, tax, real estate, probate, banking, and transactional lawyers;
- The *ABA/Unix* Newsletter, about Unix hardware and software for the Unix operating system;
- The ABA *LitApps* Newsletter, on technology for litigators.

To orient yourself further to this brave new world, check out
- *Access 1994*, edited by John C. Landis;
- The ABA LPM annual Techshow, the world's largest legal technology conference with seminars, demonstrations, and exhibits, held every March in Chicago.

Evaluating All Software

Lawyers often evaluate computer applications by price and features alone, neglecting the "little things"
- How easy is it to navigate through the program's menus and data? Every keystroke and mouse-click saps energy.
- Does the program have shortcuts? For example, GUI programs should provide key combinations that are equivalent to mouse operations. (Computers have special keys along with the regular typewriter keys. Pressing a special key at the same time as a typewriter key is a **key combination.**)
- Do the on-screen menus make sense? Can you figure out what you need to do from the menus, or must you consult the manual every time you want to do something new?
- Are the help screens helpful? Help screens should tell you what you need to know when you need it.
- Can you find what you need in the user manual easily?
- How often does it crash? (The question is not "Will it crash?" but "When?")

Unfortunately, few trade publications bother to write about the small stuff, so you're mostly on your own when checking out these little things. Any Windows application ought to be easier to use than any DOS application, but that's not guaranteed.

Try Before You Buy

Always ask vendors when and how you can return their product. Mass-market software you buy from a retail store usually isn't returnable, but you can often buy mass-market software direct from the vendor with a 30 to 90 day return policy. Legal software often is returnable, but don't assume it is.

Local dealers of legal software will visit your office to demonstrate their products or invite you to test their software at their local facility. Many vendors will send you an evaluation copy of their application to try out on your own computer. An **evaluation copy** is a crippled version of the real application. For example, time/billing evaluation software limits the number of timekeepers and transactions you can enter. Evaluation copies should include extensive sample data so you can thoroughly test the program without having to do data entry.

When you request an evaluation copy, some vendors will send you a **demo disk** instead. A demo disk is merely advertising, a kind of "slide show," not the real application. Sometimes demo disks can help computerphobes get over their fear of computers.

The ABA LawTech Center in Chicago will let you do hands-on software evaluation of the products on display there, for as long as you want and without the vendor or dealer present. Call the ABA Clearinghouse (312/988-5465) for an appointment.

Additional Considerations for Legal-market Software

You cannot buy most legal-market software "off-the-shelf." You can buy it from the software vendor or from authorized dealers. Below are questions you should ask of these vendors and dealers.

How Much Does It Cost?

Books on practicing law cost more than books for the mass-market. Similarly, legal-market software costs more than mass-market software (in about the same ratio). If the application does what you want with minimal setup and training, it may be worth it to you.

Some legal software vendors charge separately for required training, support, and maintenance (essentially, fixing bugs). When comparing software for purchase, be sure to add those costs to the purchase price.

Will the Application Be Easy to Use?

Until recently legal-market applications were easier to learn and use than mass-market software. Now often the reverse is true. Ease of use for a computer program has to do with the program's **user interface.** When you run a program and look at its screen, you're looking at the computer program's user interface. You enter information into a program and tell the program what to do with it through the program's user interface.

Programs with modern user interfaces come with menus that list what you can do with the program. They have **look-up tables** (also called pop-up tables) that can list your clients, for example, so you can pick the client whose data you want to see on the screen. Modern programs use colors well. On-screen options are clear so you can avoid extensive training and constant referral to the manual.

Beware of poorly designed user interfaces, especially in older programs. In the early days, computer programs were "user-vicious." Computer programs don't have to be hard to use, even when the underlying substantive material of the application is complex.

Find out what training the vendor recommends or requires. Often the more training required, the worse the user interface, because you must learn the idiosyncrasies of badly designed software.

Will the Application Do What I Want?

An application's user interface limits what you can do with the information entered into it. If an application cannot answer a properly conceived question (and if the information exists to answer the question), the application's user interface is at fault. For example, if a case management program does not give you a simple list of your clients and their phone numbers, then the program is not doing what you want. If an application cannot perform a task you need—for example, if a docket control program cannot automatically generate calendar events as you would like—then the program is not doing what you want.

Remember that legal-market computer applications only can work within the framework discussed previously in this chapter. They usually work only on tables and text. The most these applications can do with this information is to edit, search, sort, filter, calculate, and merge.

For a simple way to check out a program's features, ask the vendor for sample reports. To analyze a program in more depth, ask the following questions:

- What tables does the application keep?
- Can I edit the information in the tables? Which tables can't be edited? (You may want some tables to be unchangeable.)
- Can I get sorted lists of information? Filtered sets of lists?
- What calculations does it do? Do I want a time/billing program to split a deposit to credit several client accounts. You may want a docket program to calculate docket events for me starting with answering the complaint through discovery and trial? Will the program do it?

Some vendors will offer to "customize" a program for you. That is, they will change the program's instructions to give you the information you want. Customization can be expensive—get a price quote up front. Some applications come with report writers that let a programmer generate "custom" reports for you.

Is the File Format Standard?

Avoid law-office software with proprietary file formats. Once you invest time and money entering data into an application, you'll be glad to know that if your vendor goes out of business, programs from other vendors can read your files.

Will Installation Be Easy?

Installing programs that will run on your desktop computer should be easy: you should be able to type in one command and expect the program to take care of the rest. However, legal-market software is sometimes complicated to install.

Network legal-market software is often hard to install. If you have a client-server network, have a LAN administrator install the software for you.

Is the Application Copy-Protected?

Because computer software is easy to pirate, sometimes law-office software is **copy-protected.** The standard copy-protection scheme makes it difficult to copy from one floppy disk to another, so you cannot conveniently copy the set of original floppy disks to other floppy disks. This scheme protects against software piracy but means you cannot exercise your right to an archival backup (making copies of your original floppy disks to use in case the originals are damaged.)

Standard copy protection has never worked well, because as soon as someone invents a copy-protection scheme, someone else writes software to circumvent it. Most software vendors have abandoned copy protection and now rely on copyright law and software license agreements.

Other copy-protection schemes include the following:

- **Dongles.** A dongle measures approximately 1¼″ by 1¼″, is attached to your parallel port, and costs about $600. Without a dongle, the software won't run. Dongles are easily stolen.

- Programs that become inoperable if you've compressed them to save space and expanded them later. This becomes inconvenient when you have a chock-full hard disk and are trying to compress programs you use infrequently.

- Although mass-market software is easy to learn from the screen—you often don't have to open the manual to learn the basics—legal-market software often is not. The cryptic screens of some legal-market software make the software useless to software pirates, because you need training and documentation to use them. This scheme isn't really copy protection, although the effect is the same.

These copy-protection schemes can be annoying, but some vendors consider them necessary. Before buying a legal-market application, ask the vendor if the application is copy-protected.

Is the Application Stable?

Independent laboratories and millions of users test mass-market software. However, legal-market software has a small **installed user base** (roughly, the number of users) and no independent laboratories to test it.

Trade magazines sometimes publicize serious flaws in mass-market software, but you'll rarely see a bad review of a legal-market application.

Can the Application Work with Other Applications?

Unless you buy integrated software from a single vendor, you cannot conveniently share information among separate programs. For example, you'll have to enter duplicate client information into docket and time/billing software from different vendors.

Many time/billing vendors offer time/billing programs that share information with the vendor's accounting system. Beware of programs advertised as "integrated" that require you to "manually" transfer electronic information from one part of the system to the other.

Some vendors advertise integrated time/billing with secondary case management, docket, and conflicts of interest modules. Often these modules have limited features.

Does the Application Work with Windows?

Most legal-market software is still DOS-based. Some DOS programs crash under Windows. Some vendors advertise "Windows-like" programs that are easier to use than older DOS applications, but these may cooperate poorly with Windows.

Windows-based legal-market software is just getting off the ground. Don't buy the first version of a Windows-based law-office program. Windows programming is difficult and takes a while to get right.

Custom Database Software

Most computer programs are off-the-shelf or available from a legal software vendor. You do not write a word processing program yourself—somebody else already has done for you.

If you hire someone to write a computer program specifically for your law office, perhaps because nothing available for sale suits you, then please note:

- The basis of the custom program should be a mass-market database. Find out which database it is, and make sure other programmers can work with it. If your programmer wants to write the program from scratch, find out why. Programs written from scratch are likely to have bugs and be maintainable only by the programmer who created them.
- Computer programming, especially Windows-based programming, is difficult and prone to error. Off-the-shelf software is widely tested. Custom software is not.
- The need to do error checking makes programming harder.
- The need to make programs user-friendly makes programming harder.
- Make sure you and your programmer determine ownership rights up front, or you may later find you bought a nonexclusive license to use the software you paid to have written, instead of the software itself.
- Finally, think hard before you spend more money in an attempt to recoup your expense by trying to market your application to other law firms (thus getting out of the business of practicing law and into the arguably far more dangerous business of selling software).

Organizing Your Law Practice with a Computer

This book advocates using mass-market solutions to automate law-office operations as much as possible. If you stick with Windows applications, you can buy them one or two at a time, as you need them, and they will all get along with each other. Once you learn to use one Windows application, it's easier to learn others, especially if they're from the same vendor.

Your computer most likely will come installed with the latest versions of MS-DOS and Microsoft Windows. If not, these programs will cost about $100 total. If you decide to use Windows, buy Windows-based applications, because they will run better under Windows than DOS-based applications will. All Windows-based applications have a Windows logo on the box.

Organizing Your Law Practice with a Computer

- Everyday documents
  - Comparison
  - Assembly
  - Management
  - Desktop publishing
  - Office suites/integrated packages
- Finance management applications
- Client matters
  - Using a flexible PIM
- Organizing litigation documents
- Automating areas of practice
- Law-related CD-ROMs
- Networking for the law office
- Online services
- Telecommunications software

Each of the following sections describes a part of your law-practice operations that you can automate separately. Each section gives a brief overview of solutions using mostly low-end mass-market software and mentions specific products suitable for that area. The summary table at the end of this chapter provides a partial product and price list. Please don't construe product references (or omissions) as recommendations by the ABA.

Automating Everyday Documents

Buy a word processor right away to handle documents you create and work with every day, such as letters, contracts, memos, and briefs. The "Big Three" of Windows word processors are Microsoft Word for Windows, WordPerfect for Windows, and Lotus AmiPro (corresponding roughly to GM, Ford, and Chrysler). Any of these programs can handle special formats such as italics, highlighting, and underlining or special features such as footnotes, endnotes, and tables of authorities and contents. If you have a special legal practice system in mind and it coordinates with a particular word processor, you'll want to buy that word processor.

A word processor will help you enormously in your law practice. You'll crank out documents faster than your nonautomated colleagues. You'll save time by making corrections on screen. (Assistants still come in handy for labor-intensive tasks you otherwise would have to do yourself, such as proofreading, printing, and mailing documents.)

Not everyone in your office needs to use the same word processor. If a lawyer, for example, is computer-literate enough to have strong product preferences, he or she should know enough to minimize the confusion that may occur when different products are used to do the same thing.

Document Comparison

You can compare different versions of the same document with most word processors. Standalone document comparison software includes CompareRite by Jurisoft.

You'll quickly find that document comparison works best with documents that have only minor differences. However, you could easily miss these minor but often critical differences if you were proofing documents without the aid of a computer.

For example, a small software company sealed its ultimate fate, bankruptcy, when the company's president and lawyers missed the addition of "for one year" in a last-minute revision to a software source code license agreement. This is a powerful argument for insisting on electronic copies of agreements during contract negotiations.

Document Assembly

A word processor can create simple form letters, such as an announcement of a move to a new office or a change in the law. However, some law practices—insurance subrogation defense and group legal services, for example—involve creating the same types of documents over and over again. Using a word processor to create these documents is tedious and error-prone. Buying a document assembly program such as HotDocs by Capsoft makes sense.

Document Management

You can attach identifying information to your word processor documents. Microsoft Word for Windows allows you to associate a title, subject, author, keywords, and comments with each document. Then, for example, you can search for all documents tagged with the keyword *brief*, or search the text of all documents for the word *asbestos.*

More sophisticated document management software includes SoftSolutions and PC-DOCS. These products are high-end mass-market products that are marketed heavily to the legal community. Such applications are useful in large, networked law offices.

Desktop Publishing

If you want to put out a simple client newsletter, a word processor will do nicely. *The Lawyer's PC* (Shepard's McGraw-Hill) is published using a Windows word processor. Desktop publishing (DTP) software becomes a necessity when you want to include images in your newsletter, such as a chart, a map, or a logo.

Traditionally, DTP software has been expensive and difficult to use. Microsoft Publisher is a program that is less expensive and easier to use than other DTP software but has fewer features. For example, Publisher does not do the color separations that printing service bureaus usually require for color printing.

Office Suites and Integrated Packages

Office suites bundle programs usually sold separately, such as a word processing program, spreadsheet program, and relational database program. If your practice involves calculations, you'll need the spreadsheet software. However, you will probably not need the relational database program right away, if ever. Microsoft, WordPerfect, and Lotus each offer office suites.

In contrast to an office suite, an integrated package combines limited word processing, spreadsheet, database, and communications capabilities into one inexpensive program. Microsoft Works, for example, is a bargain—it costs less than $100 (street price). The problem is that once you get used to the advanced features of the "grown-up" versions of software, you'll never be happy with the "baby" versions again.

Finances

In a perfect computer world you could enter a transaction and your computer software would know exactly what you wanted to do with it. For example, your entry of "Telephone conversation with George Brown; gave brief advice on domestic issue, to meet with me before acting; scheduled meeting in our office tomorrow at 9am" would appear as an appointment on your calendar, an entry in Brown's client history, and a transaction to be billed to Brown at your hourly rate. A payment from George would appear in his client history, your statement of your "bottom line," and your checking account records.

Failing that, in a perfect world, computer software would seamlessly handle everything you do that involves money, including hourly time, flat fee tasks, client expenses, office expenses, income, taxes, and your bottom line.

Unfortunately, finance is an area of automation where the piecemeal information and learning curve problems, described at the beginning of this chapter, are especially acute. You might have an integrated time/billing, trust accounting, other accounting, and payroll system, with no convenient way to combine that information with other office expenses to generate tax forms. You might have a mass-market bookkeeping program that will feed into a mass-market tax program but doesn't integrate with time/billing software.

Nonetheless, if you're swamped with business at the outset, get your bills and books automated right away. Otherwise you soon will be swamped with financial work that you'll have to handle manually. If you're setting up practice and have few clients, however, wait to invest in financial software. You've time to discover how your practice is going to develop before choosing financial software.

Mass-Market Time/Billing Software

Buy a mass-market time/billing program for professional offices. Your time/billing program should be able to handle hourly billing, task-based (flat-fee) billing, expenses, and trust accounting. It should include a timer that you can turn on and off to track time spent. Ideally, mass-market time/billing programs should be able to handle client/matters well, but they sometimes don't. TimeSlips for Windows by TimeSlips Corporation is a mass-market program popular with lawyers. TimeSlips lets you link your time/billing data to most accounting programs. Make sure your accounting program can handle cash-based accounting—many mass-market accounting programs won't. One-Write Plus Accounting from Business Services Software, Inc., handles cash-based accounting.

One expert recommends you buy the same accounting application as your accountant uses, because you can save money at tax time by giving your accountant a floppy disk containing your accounting data from the application.

Mass-Market Bookkeeping Software

If you don't need software such as TimeSlips to monitor, record, and calculate your time by the hour, consider QuickBooks for Windows, an easy-to-use bookkeeping, bill-paying, expense-tracking, invoicing, and payroll system by Intuit. Several experts in time/billing and accounting don't recommend this solution; QuickBooks has no audit trail, for example. Nevertheless, QuickBooks has worked well for me. I keep QuickBooks open all the time to record invoices and expenses as they occur. Data files from QuickBooks for Windows should soon be readable by Windows tax preparation software such as TaxCut '93 for Windows by MECA Software, Inc.

Figure 13 (page 86) shows a graph of law firm income from Quick-Books for Windows.

Legal-Market Time/Billing Software

Many legal vendors sell integrated time/billing and accounting systems, including Software Technology Inc. and Juris. These companies will provide training and support. Doing it this way will cost the most money up front.

Tracking Clients and Matters

The paperless office is a buzzword nowadays, but paperless offices are still decades away. For now, you'll need a paper-file cabinet as well as a computer. You'll have paper files from other sources. You'll want to have

Figure 13: A Graph of Law Firm Income

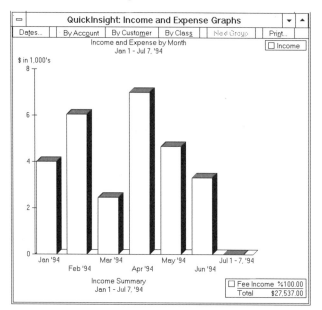

paper copies of your documents to cover yourself in case your computer crashes. You'll want to file paper copies of articles and cases. However, you'll need less paper-file space with a computer because the details that lawyers normally keep in paper-files—notes, schedules, lists of documents—are better kept in a computer.

PIMs, document managers, docket control, case management, and other types of applications are ways of getting information out of on paper form—out of your file cabinets, rolodexes, appointment calendars and the big court calendars on the wall—and into a computer where you can do a lot more with it.

Don't try any of these solutions until you've your word processing under control. Using these programs requires learning and experimenting. To start, enter data for one or two clients and explore what the program can do with those data.

Using a Flexible PIM

This section gives an overview of one way to track these details by using a mass-market PIM. Because a PIM uses the same electronic database tools that legal-market applications use, with a PIM you can do simple case management, docket/calendaring, conflicts of interest checking, and document management.

The maxim "Choose the software to fit the way you work" is right on target for PIMs. Think about what you do and how you do it by hand. How would you want this same information to look on your machine? Some users like specialized PIMs, where there is a place for everything and it's easy to put everything in its place. Others prefer a flexible PIM, which is harder to learn but gives you more control over your information. The PIM interest group of the ABA Law Practice Management Section reviews all known PIMs and can help you decide which PIM is right for you.

The examples that follow come from ECCO, a flexible PIM by Arabesque Software, and include client data adapted from the legal practice template included with ECCO.

Tracking Clients, Cases, and Contacts

A PIM can keep an electronic phone book of your clients and other contacts, as shown in figure 14.

You can autodial with most PIMs if your phone system can handle a modem connection. (Any modular home phone outlet can handle a modem.) When you use **autodialing,** the PIM instructs your modem to dial the number for you. When a connection is established, you pick up the telephone attached to the modem and talk.

Figure 14: An Electronic Phone Book

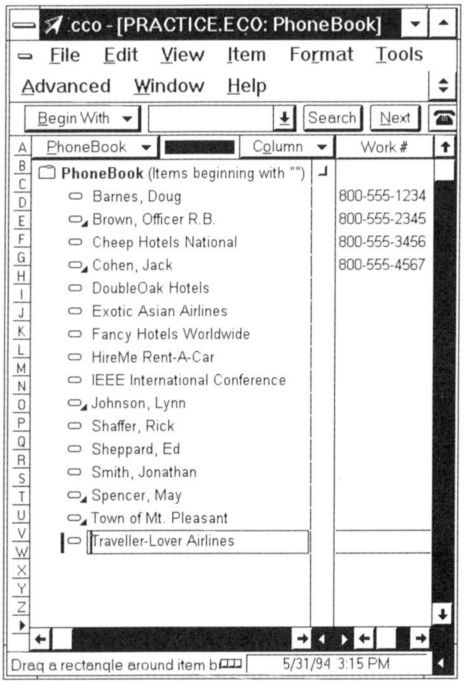

Figure 15:
Client History

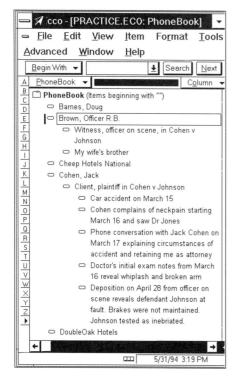

Figure 16:
Document Descriptions
and File name

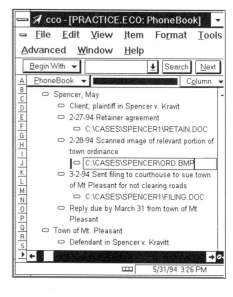

With a PIM, you can send a contact's address information to a word processing program to write a letter, then to a label printer to print a label for the envelope.

Keeping on Top of Conflicts of Interest

You can enter into your PIM the name and description of every person and company who might present a conflict of interest to you. Your description should include your relationship with this person or company. Your phone book will become huge quickly. Some PIMs will let you hide names you don't want to see routinely.

Keeping Client Histories

Good PIMs let you keep notes on your clients and other contacts. You can put dated descriptions of client transactions in the client's notes, in chronological order. Types of transactions could include, for example,

• "left message" notes;
• date and time of long distance calls;

- advice given;
- meeting notes;
- the text of electronic mail you send to and receive from your staff, your clients, and your colleagues;
- the text of other correspondence.

If you have a portable computer, you can take notes with your PIM when you're at court or at a client's site.

If you enter notes on all client transactions, including time spent, into your PIM, then you will have in one place a complete set of searchable and classifiable records of what you've done for a client. If you write notes on scraps of paper, be diligent about entering these notes into your PIM later so you can retrieve them easily. (However, keep the scraps of paper around, even if you just throw them into a drawer. At some point, you may have to show these notes to a court or reconstruct an electronic file from them.)

If you have a color monitor on your computer, you can use color to flag clients and client notes you want to stand out. For example, you can highlight the name of a nonpaying client in red. Figure 15 shows a record of client's history.

Organizing Client Documents

PIMs allow you to include the file names of documents in your client histories. For example, suppose you've prepared a trial memorandum. You've named your document *trialmem.doc*, a necessarily cryptic DOS file name. You can create an item that describes the document and put the file name under this item. You can launch (run) the word processing program that created the file, edit it, and return to the PIM when you're done. (This is a way to create a simple mass-market document management system.)

Figure 16 shows examples of document descriptions and file names created for a client. You can also keep track of other client files, such as spreadsheets and images, this way.

Appointments and Things to do

You can add appointments, including docket events, and tickler ("things to do") items to a calendar and display them by month, day, and week. Figure 17 (page 90) shows an electronic version of a daytimer.

With some PIMs, you can display "to-do" items as a Gantt chart, a bar

Figure 17: Daytimer

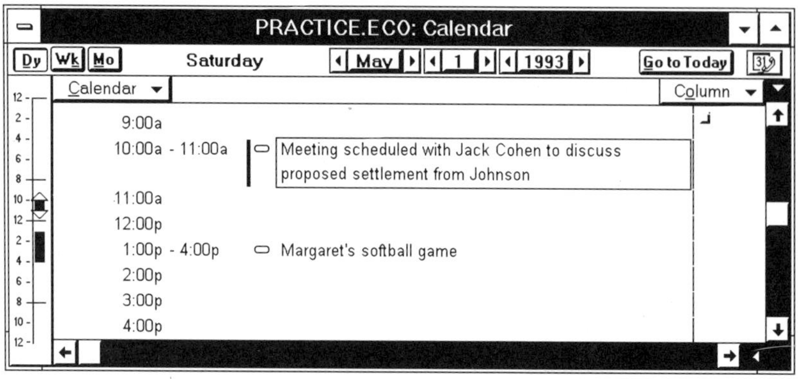

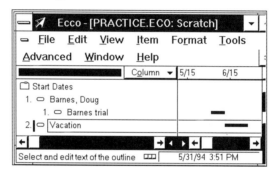

Figure 18: Gantt Chart

chart that shows these items over time. Figure 18 (above) shows a few "to do" items displayed as a Gantt chart.

Organizing Miscellaneous Text

You can implement most of the above with ECCO Simplicity 2.0, a $100 PIM (list price). With the complete version of ECCO Professional 2.0 (list price $280), you can also track miscellaneous pieces of text such as the following:

- Boilerplate contract clauses that you can assign to electronic file folders you create, such as "jurisdiction" and "term." Then you can use the ECCO "shooter" function to send these clauses into a word processing program, edit them into a contract, and save the completed contract as a separate document file.
- Case law abstracts.
- Interrogatory questions.
- Witnesses and abstracts for litigation.

You can set up an ECCO view containing an "information bank" of briefs, interrogatories, and other documents. If you're on a local area network, you can make this information available to other network users of the same PIM.

Finances

Eventually, PIMs will take on spreadsheet functions—they will become good at doing arithmetic. Then it may become practical to keep all time and expense transactions in one PIM file and run your billing and tax programs from there. For example, with some PIMs you can automatically log the time spent on telephone calls.

Legal-Market Solution

Mass-market programs can keep track of appointments and docket events. However, it's more cost-effective to buy a program that can automatically generate docket events from court rules than to try to replicate this function with mass-market software. Abacus Law is a popular and inexpensive DOS-based docket control program that also enables you to track clients, matters, and events.

Organizing Litigation Documents

In litigation, you can be easily overwhelmed by both electronic files and paper-files. You may have hundreds of megabytes of electronic interrogatories, depositions, and trial transcripts. You may have boxes upon boxes of papers annotated with handwritten scribbles, some of them crucial and others trivial. The goal of automating litigation documents is to separate the wheat from the chaff, to make bringing in the sheaves, so to speak, easier.

Full-Text Searching

Often you can accomplish what you need to do in a case by searching on a single word or two in your collection of documents in text form. A solo practitioner in Washington State recently settled a case in his client's favor when he found the words "kitchen sink" in one of the computer transcripts for his case.

Your word processor and utilities such as Central Point PC Tools for Windows or Norton Desktop for Windows can search one or more files for a single word or phrase. Mass-market applications with indexed search and retrieval capabilities include (1) search and retrieval software such as Zyindex for Windows and (2) document management software such as SoftSolutions and PC DOCS.

Imaging

Use an optical scanner to capture paper documents as images in electronic files, to preserve handwritten notes. Then use a flexible PIM such as ECCO (described above) to describe, classify, and launch the file names of these image files.

Legal-Market Solution

Legal-market litigation support software can perform complex indexed searches on large litigation text files, display hits, and keep abstracts and notes. These programs provide a systematic way to do the same tasks paralegals have traditionally done manually.

Automating a Substantive Area of Your Practice

Substantive software automates practice areas such as corporate counsel, plaintiff's personal injury, real estate, bankruptcy, estate planning, and the corporate secretary.

Mass-Market Solutions

You can automate any substantive area of your practice with mass-market software. You can create any legal form you need with a word processor, such as bankruptcy, real estate, and matrimonial law. You can do any calculations you need with a spreadsheet. For example, matrimonial lawyers can use spreadsheets to calculate divisions of assets with different percentages. You can keep any database you need with mass-market database software.

Legal-Market Solutions

The advantage of legal-market applications is that good ones will take you through the steps you need to automate a substantive area and remind you what documents you need to be keeping. In the future, more of these systems will also incorporate knowledge of legal experts.

An old PC, such as a 286, that's useless for running Windows software, comes in handy for running legal-market applications. Most of these programs are DOS-based and will run well on older machines.

CD-ROMs

The *Directory of Law-Related CD-ROMs* is a printed reference of all legal CD-ROM products, updated quarterly (available from Infosources Publishing, 201/836-7072).

Legal-market CD-ROMs can be expensive. Subscriptions to some CD-ROM services cost $2000 to$4000 a year. CD-ROM services make sense if you work in one area of law, tax law, for example, because you can easily spend more on online research. Matthew Bender, West, and Commerce Clearinghouse are three major CD-ROM vendors.

Low-End Networking

Methods to share electronic information and resources such as printers with other computer users in your law office range from simple, low-cost methods to complicated, expensive ones. Below are a few easy ways to share information and resources without breaking the bank.

SneakerNet

SneakerNet is a slang term. You copy a document you're working on from your hard disk to a floppy disk and deliver it to someone else (no matter what kind of shoes you wear) to read on their computer.

SneakerNet is a cheap, convenient way to share electronic files occasionally. The more files you want to share, however, the more inconvenient SneakerNet will become.

Attaching Several Computers to One Printer

You can buy inexpensive devices that let several users share one printer. Multishare, by Linksys, is a printer-sharing device that lets up to 24 PCs share up to eight printers; printers may be placed up to 1200 feet away. It will cost about $150, plus $50 for each PC and printer.

Fast network laser printers make sense for long print jobs, but to save time and frustration, consider buying each computer user an inexpensive inkjet printer, such as the Hewlett-Packard 500 (less than $300) for small print jobs such as letters and memoranda. In the author's experience, printers are like photocopy machines—they break down just when you need them most.

Simple Inexpensive Networks

The Coactive Connector is a simple way to install a network in your office. It costs about $100 to $150 per PC ($30 per Macintosh), including both hardware and software, and can connect up to 32 computers and printers. Coactive users can access the hard disks of other Coactive computers and they can share printers.

Each computer on the network runs Coactive software. Coactive hardware plugs into the parallel port of each computer on the network. Telephone cords (the same as on a home phone) run between them in a daisy-chain (Figure 19).

Like other networks, each computer on the Coactive network can be a different species, such as a PC or a Macintosh, or can use a different PC processor, such as a 386, 486, or Pentium. Network users can access the hard disks of other network computers. Figure 20 shows the Windows file manager, running on a PC, displaying files on a Macintosh hard disk that is on the same Coactive network as the PC.

The advantage of the Coactive network is that you can easily install it yourself, even if you're a computer novice. The disadvantage is that it's

Figure 19: A Coactive Network

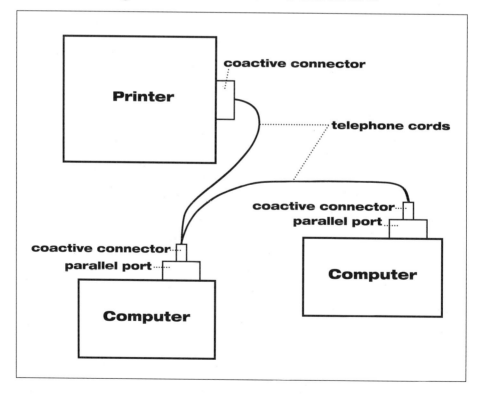

Figure 20:
File Manager Display of Files
on a Coactive Network

```
┌─────────────────────────────────┬─────────────────────────────────┐
│ ─ File Manager - N:\CAROL\* ▼   │ ─ File Manager - N:\MAC.MA ▼  ▲ │
├─────────────────────────────────┼─────────────────────────────────┤
│ File  Disk  Tree  View          │ File  Disk  Tree  View          │
│ Options  Window  Help           │ Options  Window  Help           │
├─────────────────────────────────┼─────────────────────────────────┤
│ ─ a  ─ b  c  d  n               │ ─ a  ─ b  c  d  n               │
│ x              n:[coacti        │ x              n:[coactive]      │
├─────────────────────────────────┼─────────────────────────────────┤
│ n:\          !network           │ n:\          !1col_au.ep        │
│   carol      private            │   carol      !computr.ep        │
│     !network !2_col_p           │   mac.mac    !legal-a.eps       │
│     private  !altshif           │              !phomnic.ep        │
│   mac.mac    foog               │              !viewpla.eps       │
│              !1col_au.eps        │              asa.eps            │
├─────────────────────────────────┼─────────────────────────────────┤
│ N: 46.2MB free, 115MB total Total│ N: 46.2MB free, 115MB total Total│
└─────────────────────────────────┴─────────────────────────────────┘
```

slow. Lantastic (Artisoft) or Windows for Workgroups (Microsoft) are faster network products, but are more expensive and harder to set up than the Coactive Network, partly because you must install a network card inside each computer on the network.

If your law firm must share information, such as a time/billing database or e-mail, and speed of information transfer is critical, then investigate a "client server" network. Hire a network provider to select and install the network for you and be prepared to spend a lot of money. Your best bet is a Novell network because Novell currently has a huge market share, but other networks are available. Choose a network provider as you would choose a computer consultant (see chapter 2).

Online Services

You can send e-mail inexpensively through commercial online services such as CompuServe, ABA/net and America Online. However, while the e-mail programs on a LAN won't notify you automatically when you receive mail, you must remember to check your online services routinely for new electronic mail.

Online services run on remote computers (in another location). Unlike the Westlaw or LEXIS computerized legal research services, the content of these online services comes mainly from its users, not the service provider. Your computer connects to an online service through a telephone line and your modem. These services come in especially handy when you're away from the office and want to send or receive mail in the middle of the night.

These online services are a big part of what people call the "Information Highway." Other online service facilities include

- attaching electronic files to e-mail. When you're away from your office, you can e-mail a note to your assistant and attach a long document you created with your word processor. (This procedure is easier than trying to connect with your office computer from a remote site.)
- sending electronic faxes. These work like e-mail, but the message is printed on the recipient's fax machine.
- computer conferencing, a way to hold electronic conversations on particular topics. Conversations are recorded and preserved for other online users to read and add to. Commercial software vendors often provide technical support to users through computer conferences. Participants in these conferences treat novice users kindly.
- access to **shareware** (software sold on a "try it and buy it if you like it" basis). Individuals, not companies, usually write shareware and **upload** it to online services. When you're connected to the online service, you can download the shareware to your computer. The best computer games are shareware, but finding good shareware involves culling through hundreds of shareware offerings.
- gateways to reference services such as Dialog and NewsNet. A **gateway** gets you from one service to another. For example, ABA/net has gateways to Westlaw and LEXIS.

Some commercial online services can send and receive Internet electronic mail. The **Internet** is a loose conglomeration of online services and resources. Large private companies, government agencies, and universities receive e-mail through the Internet. If you work for one of these organizations, Internet access may be free for you.

The Internet offers access to electronic libraries worldwide. For example, you can retrieve legal materials, such as U.S. Supreme Court opinions, through the Internet. Services such as Delphi and hundreds of small local service bureaus provide paid access to these Internet resources. For example, a small service provider in Chicago charges $25 per month for unlimited access to the Internet.

The Internet offers e-mail but no convenient way to find any Internet user's e-mail address. On the Internet you can access computer conferences on topics from programming languages and TV shows to topics you would not want your children to see, but the software to access these conferences is cumbersome. In fact, all current Internet software is not especially user-friendly, but it promises to get better in the next year or two. To help you onto the Internet, the ABA will soon publish *Internet in One Day*, by G. Burgess Allison.

Communications Software

Most commercial online services, including CompuServe, America Online, ABA/net, Westlaw and LEXIS, will sell you Windows-based communications software to connect to them. Microsoft Windows also comes with an adequate low-end communications program, called Terminal.

If you buy a **fax modem** (a modem that can send and receive faxes), low-end **fax software** to do electronic faxing from your PC usually comes with it. More elaborate fax software exists, such as WinFax Pro by Delrina.

If you plan to use your modem frequently, consider installing a second telephone line that not part of an office phone system. Make sure this line doesn't have call-waiting.

Summary of Applications

Table 13 (page 98) shows a partial product and price list for software mentioned in this chapter. These prices are list price, which is full retail. If you shop around, you can buy these products at a far lower street price, often half of the list price.

Table 13: Products and prices

Chapter 9 Section	Product Category	Windows Mass-Market Applications	Legal-Market Applications
Everyday documents	Word processing	Word processors: Microsoft Word, $500 Word Perfect, $500 Lotus AmiPro, $500	
	Document comparison	CompareRite (Jurisoft), $190	
	Document assembly	HotDocs (CapSoft), $50	
	Document management	SoftSolutions for Windows, $300-$600 PC DOCS $230-$300	
	Office suites	Borland Office (includes Word Perfect, Paradox, Quattro Pro), $600 Lotus SmartSuite (includes Lotus 123, Freelance Graphics, AmiPro, Organizer, Approach), $800 Microsoft Office (includes Word, Excel, PowerPoint, license for Microsoft Mail), $750	
	Integrated packages	Microsoft Works for Windows, $140 PFS, $120 ClarisWorks, $250	
	Desktop publishing	Microsoft Publisher, $200 Aldus Pagemaker, $900	
	Slide show presentations	Lotus Freelance Graphics, $500 Microsoft PowerPoint, $500	
Litigation documents	File utilities	Central Point PC Tools for Windows, $180 Norton Desktop for Windows, $180	
	Search and retrieval	Zyindex for Windows, $400	
	Litigation support		Discovery Pro for Windows, $1200 BRS Search, $3000-$12,000
Finances	Spreadsheet	Borland Quattro Pro, $100 Lotus 123, $500 Microsoft Excel, $500	
	Time/billing	TimeSlips for Windows, $100-$300	TABS III, $500-$3,500 Juris, $3,250-$30,000
Tracking your cases	PIM	Arabesque ECCO, $100-$280 Commence, $400 Lotus Organizer, $150 Packrat, $400	
	Case management and docket control		Abacus Law, $400
Substantive areas	Variously called case management systems and substantive systems		Numerous legal-market systems ranging from a few hundred to a few hundred thousand dollars.
Online services	Communications software	ProComm for Windows, $180	

* Source for list price data: DataSources, Ziff-Davis Publishing, 1994. Prices have been rounded upward.

Chapter 10

Getting Hands-On Experience

Getting Hands-on Experience
- Computer reference materials
- Keyboard and mouse
- Using the screen
- Tutorials
- Handling electronic information
- Advanced features

O ne school of thought says you can be computer-literate without using a computer. Another school says you must get your hands dirty by placing them firmly but flexibly on a keyboard. Regardless, you personally will never be able to get anything out of a computer unless you learn how to use it yourself. Spend at least a few days to set things up and to become familiar with your hardware and software.

Learning to Use Computer Reference Materials

You may not like the manuals that come with your computer products. If you don't, go to a discount bookstore and look for books with titles like *PC's for Non-Nerds*, *Windows For Dummies*, and *WordPerfect Made Simple*. (To paraphrase Dave Barry, these titles are not made up.) Give yourself time to browse, to pick out one you'll be happy with.

Questions Everyone Asks at Some Point

- How do I turn my computer on? Your computer manual will show you the location of the power switch. If you've lost the manual, look for a power switch on one of the four sides of the computer. It could be a button on the front, a switch on one of the sides, or a switch on the back. The switch is often labeled "Power." Otherwise, look for a switch with a 0 and a 1 on it. The 0 means "power off" and the 1 means "power on."

- What and where is the "any" key? When a computer asks you to press any key, press the big key marked ENTER. (There are 101 other keys you could press, and about 91 of them would also be an acceptable "any" key.) If someone or something tells you to press the "return" key, it means to press the ENTER key.

> **Question.** *A lawyer went shopping for a "how-to" book on a popular word processor. When he saw that the smallest "how-to" book was 1-1/2" thick, he left the store, never to return. What misconception plagues this lawyer?*
>
> **Answer.** Unlike law school case books, you don't read computer manuals and help books from beginning to end, page by excruciating page. Instead, read the first chapter or two, go through the short tutorials, and quickly scan the rest of the book to see what is there, so you can refer back to it as you need it.
> Better yet, look to the ABA LPM to continue its popular "In One Hour" series, which began with *WordPerfect in One Hour for Lawyers,* by Gerald J. Robinson.

Learning to Use the Keyboard and the Mouse

Inexpensive user-friendly pen-based computers and voice-recognition devices may come to market in a few years, but for now, you must learn to use a computer keyboard to use computer software. Fortunately, you don't need to learn to use it particularly well. The computer can correct many of your mistakes. Get over the notion that if you type well you're doing clerical work. If typing is agony for you, buy a typing-tutor program and learn to type properly.

To get used to the mouse, play Windows Solitaire, a software game that comes with Microsoft Windows, until using the mouse becomes second nature.

Getting Used to the Computer Screen

Many computer-literate people still print their documents, edit the printout, and enter corrections into the computer. In the interest of productivity, efficiency, and the forests of the world, learn to find and correct your mistakes on the screen. A graphical user interface and a good monitor will help. Once you get used to it, reviewing and editing on the screen is much faster than working with paper.

Learning to Use a Product

Give yourself and your assistant time to learn a new product, even if you have to pay your assistant overtime for the weekend. Colleges and computer stores offer training on PCs, DOS, Windows, word processors, and spreadsheets. Take training just before you start to use the product, not a long time before.

Go through the product's tutorial carefully. Do each step on the computer just as the manual says. Make certain you understand what each step does before you go to the next. When you're done, you should understand the basics of the program. If the product's tutorial confuses you, try a "how-to" book. A popular publisher of these books is Sybex.

Whether you take formal training or do it yourself, play around with the product on your own. Find out what the menu options do. Read the help screens. Don't be afraid to explore—you won't break anything. Nonetheless, wait to enter critical information into your program until that lost look in your eyes has gone away.

Getting Used to Handling Electronic Information

Sometimes electronic information slips away and is hard to get back. You may delete a paragraph in a document without realizing it. You may delete a client's document directory without realizing it. Keep backups of your computer files (see Appendix A), and don't throw away your paper-files.

Computers Should Make for Less Busywork, Not More

Learning advanced features of a product can save you from busy work. If you type the same thing repeatedly, look at a product's macro feature. Macros let you associate one key-combination with many keystrokes, such as your signature. If you use WordPerfect word processing software, check out *WordPerfect Shortcuts for Lawyers: Learning Merge and*

Macros in One Hour, an ABA LPM publication by Carol L. Schlein, current chair of the LPM Computer Division.

If you create wills or other form documents, look at a word processor's mail-merge feature. If you create documents for publication, investigate a word processor's style feature.

Sometimes the simplest thing will elude you for weeks. I had difficulty scrolling page by page in Microsoft Word page layout format, until I discovered the small but obvious buttons on the lower right of my screen.

If you find yourself thinking "There has got to be a better way to do this!" there probably is. If you explore your computer manual or help screens to find a better way, you'll save hours of time and frustration in the end. The next time you go exploring, you'll find what you want more easily.

Chapter 11

A Brief Account of the PC Revolution

To people in the computer business, the computer marketplace—a loose conglomeration of hardware manufacturers, makers of specialized parts, software vendors, trade magazines, service providers, and technophiles—is a fascinating place. To people who want to use computers but who have lives outside the computer world, the computer marketplace can be overwhelming and frustrating.

> **A Brief Account of the PC Revolution**
> - In the beginning . . . mainframes and minis
> - The Apple
> - The IBM PC
> - MS-DOS
> - The first GUI—Apple Macintosh
> - Microsoft Windows
> - The problem of piracy

Knowing something about how the computer marketplace evolved is background information that any persons calling themselves computer-literate should know. A complete history of the PC Revolution would take volumes. This brief account merely touches on the highlights of the last decade and a half. Of necessity, this account omits material that many technophiles consider crucial.

The Old Days

Before the late 1970s, there were no desktop computers, only mainframe and mini-computers manufactured by large companies such as IBM. (**Mainframe computers** are huge computers requiring large rooms and massive air-conditioning. Minicomputers are smaller mainframe computers. Today, if you buy a desktop computer, you'll have a computer more powerful than any machine from the old days.) Unless you worked at an institution rich enough to buy and manage one of these monsters, you got by (just fine) without a computer.

In the old days, you needed computer programmers to get anything out of the computer. These programmers usually worked for a separate, sometimes stodgy and overly political Management Information Systems Department (MIS), or its academic equivalent, the campus computer center.

In the old days, things were much more carefully controlled than they're today. Institutions purchased hardware and software from one company that also provided support and maintenance. While institutional computer users could ignore equipment cost and maintenance worries, they paid dearly for every second of computer time they used.

The Apple

The PC Revolution began in the late 1970s when Steve Wozniak and Steve Jobs formed Apple Computer, Inc., to manufacture and sell a small desktop computer, the Apple computer. The Apple enabled anyone with tenacity and a spare $2000 to $3000 to put a computer on his or her desk. Other companies made desktop computers, but the Apple was the one of the first desktop computers to make it big time.

Third-party developers soon produced off-the-shelf computer software for the Apple. Apple users could use word processing software to produce documents. They could keep simple databases such as mailing lists. However, the invention of VisiCalc, the first spreadsheet, made the Apple especially useful to business users.

The combination of the Apple computer and third-party applications allowed users to bypass the MIS department for automation tasks and to work at home. Predictably, MIS departments responded by attempting to gain political control of the desktop computers proliferating elsewhere in their companies.

The IBM PC

Around 1981, a "maverick" IBM division in Boca Raton, Florida, came out with the first IBM desktop computer, the IBM PC, and a little later, the IBM PC/XT. A few years later, IBM introduced the IBM PC/AT to the marketplace . The IBM PC/XT was based on the "8086" processor chip by Intel; the PC/AT on its successor chip, the "80286."

The AT computer quickly became an industry standard, and anyone could make a computer like it. With the introduction of the IBM PC/AT, the business computer marketplace exploded. Consumers could choose from an enormous and confusing variety of hardware and software. The concurrent introduction of quiet, fast, and inexpensive laser printers helped make these computers successful in the business world.

MS-DOS

MS-DOS, published by Microsoft Corporation, was and still is the operating system for the PC/AT computer and its descendants. MS-DOS was arguably intended to be a toy operating system for toy computers. For example, MS-DOS programs have limited space in which to run. This problem, called *RAM-cram*, resulted from an understandable but shortsighted design decision. Changing a design decision of this magnitude is effectively impossible, because all third-party software using the operating system must be changed, too.

Several manufacturers have come out with more powerful operating systems poised to replace MS-DOS, including IBM OS/2, Microsoft Windows NT, and NextStep by NeXT Computer, Inc.

The Apple Macintosh

Users of DOS-compatible computers were stuck with a command line interface. In 1984 Apple came out with the Macintosh computer, the first commercially successful computer with a graphical user interface (GUI).

The Macintosh was technically superior to the PC/AT. For one thing, Apple designed the Macintosh to run as a GUI computer. Apple was the only company manufacturing the Macintosh, so it could maintain strict quality control. Apple encouraged Macintosh programmers to follow strict standards, to ensure all Macintosh software was consistent and easy to use. Macintosh users did useful work without the hassle of DOS-compatible computers.

Microsoft Windows

Although it tried hard in the courts, Apple Computer failed to prevent other companies from using a Macintosh-like GUI. In 1990 Microsoft Corporation released Windows 3.0, computer software featuring a Macintosh-like

GUI on the PC. (Many considered Windows 3.0 to be a **beta-test product,** a product still being tested by a select group of end-users and not ready for market yet.) In 1991 Microsoft released Windows 3.1, a vastly improved version.

How the PC Marketplace Settled Out

The monopoly that Apple exercised over the Macintosh kept it from being wildly successful in the business world. By the late 1980s, the computer marketplace had settled out. DOS-compatible computers were the most popular desktop computers in the business world, and MS-DOS was the operating system that ran them. The Macintosh ran a distant second in business environments. This is still true.

Modern Pirates

The computer industry considers software piracy a major hassle. Computer software has always been easy to pirate. All you need is a computer with a floppy disk drive to copy the software diskettes and a photocopy machine to copy the documentation. Copy protection, which makes software difficult to copy from one floppy disk to another, has never worked particularly well because as soon as someone invents a copy-protection scheme, someone else writes software to circumvent it.

Eventually, most software publishers gave up on copy- protection schemes because they're mostly ineffective and cause more trouble than they're worth. Nowadays publishers rely on copyright law and the software's license agreement to protect them. License agreements typically have provisions prohibiting, in effect, the following activities:

- You buy a shrink-wrapped word processing program for $300 from a local computer store. You install it on your office computer and then you take it home to install it on your family computer.
- You buy the same program, install it on your office computer, and then lend it to your assistant to install on his or her computer.
- Your billion-dollar company buys one legitimate copy of a good product from a small software publisher. It makes 400 pirated copies and distributes them internally, aware that the small software publisher cannot afford the cost of enforcing the license agreement.

Software license agreements also state that the software is not guaranteed to do anything for you, despite all the ad promises and all the enticing language on the shrink-wrapped box containing the software. If the software ruins your life or your business, that's your problem.

In fairness, the computer industry probably needed this kind of language to get off the ground. It's doubtful the industry would have been so successful if it had been unable to discourage at least some piracy or if it had been overrun by warranty lawsuits.

Companies are starting to audit their internal software use, and computer software companies are banding together in trade associations to fight piracy. Some experts believe that the time has also come for the software industry to take more responsibility for its products.

Computer Democracy

The PC Revolution put small computers on the desks of ordinary consumers for business and household use. Computer users can experiment with these computers without a big computer budget, without depending on computer professionals, and without worrying about computer time.

The PC Revolution changed computer hardware and software from esoteric products to ordinary consumer goods governed by the rules of the consumer marketplace. Arguably, it altered the balance of power among individuals, small companies, and large companies by giving everyone an affordable lever to retrieve and push around electronic information.

The PC Revolution has been bad news for computer companies that spent billions of dollars on proprietary technology to gain a lock on the PC marketplace. The PC Revolution has been good news for consumers, because they can buy a variety of computer hardware and software at attractive prices.

What Now?

The PC marketplace has innumerable choices, absorbing complexities, exciting products, and some of the most interesting politics around. To a computer enthusiast, it's a wondrous place. To anyone else who is trying to automate, it can be a nightmare.

I bought what I believed was the right kind of computer for her law practice in the mid-1980s, a "fat Mac," available only from Apple Computer. There was exactly one choice in the product line, the computer was a snap to set up, came with clear documentation, and included easy-to-use word processing and communications programs adequate for my needs.

Later, I added an inexpensive spreadsheet/database program to do the books. The computer performed flawlessly for four years with little maintenance and no hassles. However, unable to upgrade the Macintosh without considerable expense, I succumbed to PC mania in 1988. My old Macintosh computer is now obsolete and there is nothing else on the market like it.

Lawyers need powerful computers and software that approach being as uncomplicated, easy to set up and friendly as my old dinosaur and that are available from several sources. The PC world is getting there, but it has a way to go.

Tending to Your Computer

This chapter contains information on tasks you may want to delegate to a computer-literate assistant. It's not a complete computer maintenance course, but an attempt to put answers to frequently asked questions in one place.

Technical Support

Computer hardware and software companies usually have telephone support for their users, either an 800 number, a regular number, or sometimes a 900 number. Make sure you've the serial number for your product handy when you call technical support. When you call technical support, you may have a long wait. To make these waits bearable, buy a speaker phone or a telephone headset.

Keep the cards and boxes that come with computer equipment. You'll need the registration card to register for your warranty and free support. Always register your products. It's your only hope that the vendor will let you know about future products, and it may be required for telephone support. One of the other cards will have your product's model and serial number. You'll need the product's packaging to send the product back for return or repair.

Keep all your sales receipts, too. Some vendors require that you send in a copy of your sales receipt for special upgrade offers. Also, you may need these receipts for an IRS audit.

Hardware

Where to Put Your Computer

- Put the computer monitor and keyboard where you do your work, not off to the side. The mouse should be next to your keyboard. Leave room for papers and books.

- The computer case and its contents can go elsewhere, like on the floor. Make sure you can reach the floppy drives, power switch, and reset button easily. Position the computer so you can easily reach the back of it.
- Put the monitor where light from a window won't reflect on the screen.

You can use a large object, such as a huge vase or a large artificial plant to hide cords and cables. Don't buy a real plant unless you're completely confident that neither you nor anyone else will spill water onto the nearby computer.

If you need to dismantle equipment to move it around, label your cables and where they connect so you can reconnect them easily.

Assembling Your Computer

Keep the papers and manuals that came with your computer. They tell you how to connect the computer, keyboard, and monitor, and how to plug in equipment. If you can hook up a stereo or a VCR, you can assemble a computer.

What Are the Messages That Come Up on the Monitor When I Turn on the Computer?

These are messages from the computer system while it's booting up (starting up). Look for messages informing you of problems: they usually have the words *ERROR* or *WARNING* in them. If possible, print (with the Print Screen key) or write the error messages on a piece of paper, and have the paper handy when you call technical support for your computer.

Electrical Power Tips

Experts disagree about whether you should leave your computer powered on all the time. Recent scuttlebutt says it's OK to turn modern (circa post 1990) equipment off when you go home. However, a friend of mine recently lost the use of a state-of-the-art SCSI disk drive when he left it powered off for a few weeks. (Luckily, turning the SCSI drive on its end for a few hours got it working again.)

A screen saver program displays an ever-changing picture on your computer's monitor to prevent "burn-in." Screen savers are unnecessary for modern monitors. They're fun to use, but the I've found that some of them cause my computer to crash.

If your portable computer is powered by a nickel cadmium (nicad) battery, then before recharging it, let the battery power drain completely by leaving the battery in the computer and leaving the computer on. Recharging partially charged batteries, the theory goes, creates a false memory in the battery.

Assembling a Computer Survival Kit

Your computer should arrive with all the parts it needs. Below are supplies that will come in handy if you want to try your hand at simple computer maintenance.

- At the hardware store, buy a container of 10 to 12 small plastic trays to store small miscellaneous pieces of hardware such as jumpers and screws.
- Also at the hardware store, buy a small flat screwdriver, a small Phillips-head screwdriver, and a larger reversible screwdriver.
- At a computer store, buy a set of plastic computer screws so you'll have extra screws when you lose yours. If you can find it separately, buy a screw "grabber," so you can easily retrieve screws you've dropped onto the motherboard.
- At the computer store you can buy expensive plastic floppy disk containers that lock. Using a shoe box and rubber bands also works.

Simple Fixes

Complicated-looking problems often have simple solutions. Make sure your computer and all its devices are plugged in and turned on. If your computer freezes (stops working), press the Ctrl-Alt-Del key combination. If your computer won't reboot, press the computer's reset button if it has one; otherwise turn the computer off, wait a few seconds, and turn it back on.

Common Mistakes

Here are some mistakes made by novice—and sometimes even expert—computer users:

- Inserting a 5¼″ floppy disk the wrong way. You won't be able to use the disk inserted that way, but you won't hurt anything either.
- The computer won't let you insert a 3½″ floppy disk the wrong way.
- Bending, folding, or mutilating floppy disks.
- Letting magnets get close to your computer screen. They will cause visible interference on some screens, like making a corner of the screen yellow.

- Using brute strength on a computer. If parts don't come apart easily, pause, take a deep breath, and try to figure out why. For example, computer parts are often held together by screws, so you'll need to unscrew the screws to make the parts separate.

Likely Malfunctions

- If your computer breaks down, the hard disk drive is most likely the problem. If a hard disk is going to crash, it will most likely crash during the warranty period. Take the computer back to the dealer and insist on a new hard disk. (If your hard disk has crashed, you've lost all the information in it. This is why backing up your hard disk—making a duplicate of its contents on another hard disk or on tape—is so important. See the section on backing up files later in this chapter.)
- If your computer crashes randomly, you may have defective memory chips. Try to remember what you were doing with the computer before it crashed. See if you can cause it to crash again the same way. Then you can take the computer to your dealer and show him or her that the computer is malfunctioning. Otherwise, you may have to live with the problem.
- If you cannot print, most likely a piece of paper is stuck in the printer, just as paper gets stuck in photocopy machines. Use the instructions that come with the printer to remove the jammed paper.

Spilling Coffee or Soda on Your Keyboard

If you've spilled a lot of liquid on your keyboard, you might want to junk it and buy a new, dry one. If you're feeling brave, here's how to attempt to recover your wet keyboard:

- Save your work if you can, get to a DOS prompt, and turn off the computer.
- Disconnect the keyboard cable from the back of the machine.
- Turn the keyboard upside down over the trash basket and let the liquid drip out.
- Wipe the outside of the keyboard with paper towels. If you've just spilled a little bit of liquid on the keyboard, this may be sufficient to clean up the mess.
- Figure out how to remove the cover of the keyboard. You'll probably need a screwdriver to do it.
- Remove the keyboard cover and absorb the liquid inside the keyboard

with paper towels (giving new meaning to the term "quicker-picker-up-per").

- Let the keyboard dry out for a few hours.
- Put the cover back on, reconnect the keyboard, turn on the computer, and cross your fingers.

If you must drink around your computer, put your beverage in a sturdy container with a lid. Eating soup and crackers over your computer keyboard is out.

Buying Parts for Your Computer

Computer components are like other consumer goods. Sometimes components are expensive, sometimes they're cheap. Right now computer memory is relatively expensive, and hard disks are relatively cheap.

Question. The owner of a new Macintosh computer wanted to move her computer from one part of her home office to another. She decided to move the computer and the monitor separately. She tried to pull the monitor cable from its port on the back of the computer. It wouldn't budge. She pulled again. Eventually she pulled with all her might and the cable came loose. To her surprise, her computer would not work when she reassembled it. Why?

Answer. By pulling the monitor cable from the computer by brute force, she broke one of the parts in either the monitor port or the cable, or both.

Can I Take My Computer Apart and Look Inside?

Yes, but be sure to turn the computer and its devices off first. Beware of static electricity. If you touch a metal doorknob and are zapped, you've just discharged your static electricity and it's safe to open up your computer. Most computer manuals nowadays will show you how to open up your computer, so keep the manuals handy.

Once you've removed the computer's case, you can add parts to it such as an internal modem. You can add boards for an optical scanner or an external CD-ROM drive.

Cables, Lies, and Videotape

You use cables to attach devices such as printers, modems, and monitors to the ports on your computer. A cable is a large cord, about ¼ inch thick, with a connector on each end. A connector can be either male, which means it has pins on the end, or female, which means it has holes on the

Table 14: Cable Table

Device the Cable Is Used With	Name of the Cable	The Computer End of the Cable	The Device End of the Cable
Most printers	Parallel	25-Pin male	No pins or holes. Look for a long narrow tongue.
External modems	Serial	9-Pin female or 25-Pin female	9 Pin Male or 25 Pin Male
Monitors	VGA	15-Pin female	Permanently attached to the monitor. You can buy a monitor extension cable if the cable that comes with your monitor is not long enough.

If you've cables with the wrong connectors, you can make the right connections with a 9-to-25 pin converter and a gender changer, which changes a male into a female connector and vice versa.

end. Connectors can have 9 pins or holes, 15 pins or holes, or 25 pins or holes. Table 14 lists commonly used cables.

Catalog Sources for Cables and Other "Techie" Items

When you buy a printer or an external modem, the cables you'll need don't come with the equipment. You can buy them at a local computer store or through one of the catalogs listed in Chapter 4.

Strange Modem Numbers

If you use your communications program to set your modem to 8 bits, no parity, 1 stop bit, and no xon/xoff, it will usually work with any electronic BBS you dial.

Strange Switches

Some devices come with dip switches, a set of tiny white switches that you sometimes must reset to get your device to work the way you want. Keep the manual that comes with the device, because it will show you a dip-switch diagram and the switches you must flip to change the way the device works. The best dip-switch flipper is a letter opener with a narrow point.

Old Equipment

Keep your old computers around. Older computers run DOS-based legal-market software well. You can turn your old computer into, for example, a dedicated bankruptcy machine. If you can't use your old computer, don't toss it; donate it to charity instead.

Maintaining Your Files

How DOS Files Are Named

Remember that files exist on permanent storage such as floppy disks, hard disks, and CD-ROMs. Each of these forms of permanent storage is housed in a drive. Each drive has a letter to identify it to the computer. Floppy drives are usually named *a:* or *b:* Hard drives are usually named *c:* or *d:*.

In MS-DOS, file names must be in the form *aaaaaaaa.aaa*. For example, two valid MS-DOS file names are *winword.exe* and *mybook.doc*. The part before the period is the name and can be up to eight characters in length. The part after the period is the extension and can be up to three characters in length.

Common Mistakes

The root directory of every PC running the MS-DOS operating system has files and directories that never should be deleted:

- *autoexec.bat*
- *config.sys*
- any other file with the extension *.sys*
- the DOS or the MSDOS directories

The *autoexec.bat* and *config.sys* files control what programs your computer runs when it boots up (see page 50). Windows lets you edit these files (with the sysedit program).

Question. You have two files, george.doc *and* jeff.doc. *You want to rename the* george.doc *file to* jeff.doc *and the* jeff.doc *file to* george.doc *How do you do it?*

Answer. First rename george.doc to xx.doc. Then rename *jeff.doc* to george.doc. Finally, rename xx.doc to *jeff.doc*. The principle is that if you've two files you want to switch, create a third file where you can put one of the first two files temporarily. It's the same idea as switching furniture.

Making More Space for Your Files

Your hard disk is where you do most of your work, and you can easily run out of disk space unless you monitor your use of it. Keep at least 10 to 20 MB free on your hard disk. Below are tips to keep your electronic files from getting out of hand.

- Compress files you use infrequently and expand them only when you need them.
- Go through your directories and delete files you're certain you no longer need, but don't delete a file unless you know what it contains.

- Archive inactive files. **Archiving** means copying the files to floppy disk or tape and then deleting the files from your hard disk. Label each floppy disk clearly so you can remember its contents two years from now when you need it.
- As a last resort, double your storage space by using a program such as Stacker by Stac Technologies.

> **Question.** Why do computer companies and products have more than one capital letter in their names—for example, WordPerfect.
>
> **Answer.** Nobody knows, but here is a whimsical theory: In the early days of PCs, putting spaces in file names was a common mistake, albeit difficult to do. A file name with a space in it creates a mess. These squished-together company and product names remind us to avoid spaces in DOS file names.

Helpful Software

Commercial Windows utility software such as Central Point PC Tools for Windows and Norton Utilities for Windows can make file maintenance easier. For example, if you need to compress a file, the file manager utilities in Central Point Tools for Windows will do it. You can also locate a file you've "lost" on your hard disk by searching the contents of all your files. Finally, you can identify and get rid of duplicate files.

Smartdrive, a "disk-caching" program that comes with both MS-DOS and Microsoft Windows, dramatically improves hard disk performance.

Backing Up Your Files

No form of permanent storage is completely reliable. Hard disks can break down. Floppy disks can get wet. Tapes can get chewed up. All forms of permanent storage deteriorate over time. To compensate, you need to have the same information on more than one form of permanent storage. This process is called backing up. (Archiving, explained above, is not the same as backing up, because you normally delete archived files from your hard disk.) Below are several methods to back up your files:

- Tape backups. Make a complete backup of your hard disk every work night. Tape backup software can schedule these backups automatically. Rotate the tapes, so that you've backups of your hard disk from different times (like each Monday for the past seven weeks.) Keep at least one tape off-site. (If you have a tape drive, make sure it's cleaned routinely. Check the contents of your backup tapes often to make sure your tape backup system is working properly.

- Files on tape backups take time to access. Reserve a few floppy disks to store the documents you cannot live without. Keep them with you or take them home.

- Install a second hard disk in your computer at least as big as your first hard disk. Use it for backing up critical files on your first hard disk.

You should use all three of these methods.

Software

Your computer should have both 5¼″ and 3½″ floppy drives. If your computer has only one floppy drive, buy software with the correct size floppy disks. Some considerate manufacturers will include both types of disks in their packages.

When you buy software, use the Windows file manager to make copies of the originals (the floppy disks that came with the package). Install your software from these copies and put the originals away.

Viruses

A **virus** is a computer program that changes your computer's memory and hard disk in ways you don't want. You can set up virus checking software to run continually, but problems have occurred with this method. You should at least scan each new floppy you put into your computer's floppy drive for viruses. MS-DOS comes with a virus-checker. Often problems with software are blamed on viruses, when they're really bugs.

Bugs

All computer programs have bugs because programmers make mistakes when writing programs. Some programs have more bugs than others. Word for Windows version 6.0 reportedly has 600 bugs in it. Some scuttlebutt has the bug count at 6000 to 8000 bugs. Regardless, the product is usable.

A popular rule of thumb is never to buy a program with a version number that ends in a zero, such as Windows 3.0. In truth, the reliability of software with version numbers ending in zero depends on the vendor.

Some vendors are famous for revisions of software called flying upgrades or interim upgrades . For example the January 1990 interim upgrade of Word Perfect 5.2 was full of bugs, whereas the March 1990 interim upgrade was better.

Disconcerting Messages

Most computer programs produce baffling messages every so often. For example, Word for Windows 6.0 gives an ERROR! NO TABLE OF CONTENTS FOUND" message when you instruct it to compile a new Table of Contents; however, if you wait long enough, the error message will go away.

Malfunctions and Apparent Malfunctions

Occasionally your computer will stop running in the middle of what you're doing. Sometimes the computer is doing housekeeping, and if you wait a few seconds, your computer will resume doing what it did before.

Sometimes the pause is not normal and is probably caused by a bug, or far less likely, a virus. Slang expressions for this malfunctioning include *crashing*, *blowing up*, and *freezing*. To get your computer running again, first do a **warm boot** by pressing the Ctrl-Alt-Del key combination. If nothing happens, press the button marked reset on the front of the computer. If the computer has no reset button, turn the computer's power switch off, wait a few seconds, and turn it on again. (This is known as a **cold boot**.)

Question. A lawyer likes to borrow popular Windows software from his friends to try out. He gets his friends to put copies of their Windows software on floppy disks, which he copies to his computer. He then wonders why the software won't work on his machine. What is this lawyer doing wrong?

Answer. Windows software must be installed from the original floppy disks (or copies of them) for it to work properly. (This lawyer also is violating copyright law. His friends are violating both copyright law and their software license agreements.)

If your computer does not start up properly after you've done a cold boot, it may have a hardware malfunction, a corrupted *autoexec.bat* or *config.sys* file, or a virus.

A Few Windows Tips

1. You don't have to be under age 30 to use a mouse easily. If you've trouble **double-clicking** (quickly pressing the left mouse button twice so you can run Windows programs), change the mouse settings on the

Figure 21: The Windows Mouse Control Panel

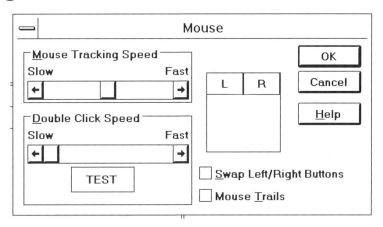

Control Panel shown in Figure 21 so that double-clicking is at its slowest rate. The Windows manual and the Windows help screens will tell you how.

2. Using the following key combinations in Windows will save time:
   • CTRL-ESC to list all programs you're running
   • ALT-TAB to go from one window to another

An Informal Glossary of Computer Terms

Access time. For permanent storage, the average time that it takes a drive to get to the information it's looking for. For temporary storage, how long it takes for a character in memory to be transferred to or from the CPU. The lower the access time, the faster the access.

Archiving. Copying inactive files to floppy disk or tape and then deleting the files from your hard disk.

ASCII format. Sometimes called text format or pure text; does not contain enhancements such as underlining, boldface, or typefaces.

Autodialing. Using software to instruct your modem to dial a phone number for you. When a connection is established, you pick up the telephone attached to the modem and talk.

Autoexec.bat. A file that tells the computer what to do when it starts up.

Backward compatibility. New software can run on older machines, albeit slowly; new software can read and write computer files from old versions of the software.

Beta-test product. A product still being tested by a select group of end-users and not ready for market yet.

Boolean search. Search <file(s)> using queries of the form "X <logical operator> Y." For example, show all the files containing both the words "murder" and "arson."

Bug. An error in a computer program.

Bus. A place on the motherboard with slots where you can insert the boards that come with some hardware devices. One way to add hardware devices to your computer.

Byte. A byte of storage holds one character, such as "a," "1," or "@."

CD-ROM drive. Reads information from CD-ROM disks.

CD-ROM. Computer disks that look like audio CD-ROM disks. They can hold a great deal of information.

Clipboard. Temporary storage used to copy data from one application to another or from one place to another within an application.

Cold boot. Turning the computer's power switch off, waiting a few seconds, and turning it on again. Also known as a cold start.

Command Line Interface. You tell the computer what to do by typing in commands.

Computer literacy. A fundamental understanding of what computers can do; having a computer on your desk and using it effectively to do your work and organize your law practice.

Computer program. See software.

Config.sys. A file that tells the computer what to do when it starts up. (Mostly used to tell the computer how to handle hardware devices attached to it.)

Copy-protection. Makes it difficult to make an unauthorized copy of software.

Cursor. A symbol on a screen showing where the next character you type will go.

Cursor keys. The keys that let you move the cursor around the screen.

Cut and paste. To transfer information within programs and from one program to another.

Data. Information to be processed by computer software.

Database. Data in table form. A mailing list is a simple database. A database can consist of one or more tables.

Database program. Computer program that processes a database.

dBASE-compatible. An industry-standard database file format.

Demo disk. A form of vendor advertising.

Desktop computer. Another term for a personal computer; also a computer housed in a case that is wider than it is tall.

Direct access. Ability to directly reach information in permanent storage.

Directory. A way to organize computer files hierarchically.

Diskette. See floppy disk.

Dongles. A device to prevent unauthorized copying of computer software. Also called a *hardware key*.

DOS-compatible. A computer that can run MS-DOS, an operating system first mass-marketed in the early 1980s by Microsoft.

Double-clicking. Quickly pressing the left button of a mouse twice.

Download. To receive a file on your computer being transmitted from another computer.

Drive. The "housing" for forms of permanent storage. For example, hard disks are housed in hard drives.

Drive bay. A place in the computer where a drive goes.

E-mail. See electronic mail.

Electronic mail. Sending and receiving messages from one computer to another. Depending on the electronic mail system, the computers can be in the same office or on the other side of the planet.

Evaluation copy. A crippled version of a real software product. For example, an evaluation copy of a time/billing program will limit the number of timekeeprs or transactions you can enter. You can get the "feel" of a program through such an evaluation copy, but you won't be able to find out how the real program handles a lot of data.

Executable. A file containing instructions that direct the computer to do a certain task, such as word processing.

External device. A device that is mostly outside the computer and usually connects to a place in the back of the computer.

Fax modem. A modem that can send and receive electronic faxes. Receives electronic image of faxes from paper fax machines.

Fax software. Software that allows you to use your fax modem to do electronic faxing from your PC.

File. A collection of data into one unit. A file might contain a letter to a client, a memo, a brief, or a spreadsheet.

File name. Every file has a name to identify it to the computer. How files are named depends on the operating system you're using.

Flat-file database. A database with one table.

Floppy disk. A form of permanent storage that serves to get information in and out of a hard disk. You insert floppy disks into a slot in the front of your computer.

Gateway. On a local area network, a way to receive electronic mail from the outside world in one place and route it to the appropriate computer on the LAN. On an online service, a way to get to another service. For example, ABA/net has gateways to Westlaw and LEXIS.

Graphical user interface. Instead of typing in a computer command, you use a mouse to select an icon or a command choice on a menu.

Graphics program. Allows you to edit images such as a photograph, a drawing, or a document scanned into the computer with an optical scanner.

GUI. See graphical user interface.

Hard disk. A form of permanent storage where you keep most of your active files.

Hardware. The computer machinery.

Hardware device. Gets information in and out of computers. Examples include drives, keyboards, mice, printers, monitors, optical scanners, and modems.

Hayes-compatible. An industry standard for modems.

Help screen. A display of text on screen that should help you understand what you're doing when you're using a computer program.

HP-compatible. An industry standard for laser printers.

Icon. A pictorial representation of a computer command.

Industry standard. A product that conforms to an industry standard follows design rules that are well-known by computer designers and programmers.

Input device. A device, such as a keyboard or optical scanner, that puts information into a computer.

Input/output device. A device, such as a disk drive or tape drive, that puts information into and gets information out of a computer.

Installed user base. Roughly, the number of users of a product.

Internal device. A device that is completely inside the computer. A hard disk is usually an internal device. A modem can be inernal or external.

Internet. A loose conglomeration of online services and resources. Previously the refuge of academics and "computer-types," in the Clinton era the Internet has become the subject of much mass-media coverage and general interest.

Key combination. Computers have special keys along with the regular typewriter keys. Pressing a special key at the same time as a typewriter key is a key combination. For example, pressing the Ctrl-Alt-Del key makes your computer do a warm boot.

Kilobyte. A kilobyte (K or KB) is 1,024 bytes.

Laser printer. A cheap and popular type of printer that uses a laser beam and metallic dust to form characters on paper. Produces documents that look typeset.

Legal-market applications. Computer applications aimed toward lawyers and law offices.

Linking. A way to tie two or more tables in a database together.

List price. Full retail.

Local area network (LAN). A way to tie PCs together to share information and resources such as a high quality printer.

Look-up tables. A predefined table of permissible values that you can "pop-up" with a mouse-click or a key combination. For example, good time/billing programs come with a look-up table of client names so you can easily select the client you want to bill a transaction to.

Macro. Lets you associate a key-combination with many keystrokes. Useful as a shortcut for entering commonly used pieces of text or series of commands.

Mainframe computer. Today, a large powerful computer. Many online services run on mainframe computers.

Mass-market application. Computer application aimed toward a wide range of computer users.

Megabyte. A megabyte (MB) is 1,048,576 (2^{20}) bytes.

MegaHertz. Millions of cycles per second. Measures processor speed.

Memory cache. Sits between RAM and the processor to make computing faster.

Menu. A list of available options in a computer program. Menus can have sub-menus, which can have sub-menus, and so on.

Microsoft Windows. A program that makes MS-DOS look like an operating system with a GUI.

Modem. A modem lets your computer communicate with another computer over telephone lines, no matter where the other computer is.

Monitor. The TV-like screen that is your view of the computer's operations.

Monochrome monitor. A monitor that displays light characters on a dark background. Usually white on black, sometimes bright green on black or amber on black.

Motherboard. Everything in your PC ultimately connects to this large greenish piece of plastic at the bottom of your PC.

Mouse. A pointing device roughly the size and shape of the animal mouse. In a graphical user interface, you use it to select icons and menu choices, which tell the computer what to do.

MS-DOS. An operating system first mass-marketed in the early 1980s by Microsoft. Still used in modern PCs. In over a decade, as gone from version 1.0 to version 6.2, no doubt its last version. Watch for another operating system to become the new standard soon, probably the one with the greatest backward compatibility.

Multimedia. Best used as an adjective to describe devices capable of displaying pictures, either still or animated, and producing sound; software capable of taking advantage of these devices; computers powerful enough to run multimedia devices and programs effectively.

Notebook computer. A type of portable computer, about the size of a medium-sized notebook and weighing 5 to 8 pounds.

OCR. See optical character recognition.

OEM. Original Equipment Manufacturer. Makes hardware sold by another company under its own name.

Online service. A computer in another location that you can connect to using a computer, a modem, and a telephone line. Provides access to e-mail and information resources. On some services, such as Westlaw, LEXIS, and Dialog, the content comes from the service provider. On other services, such as CompuServe and America Online, the content comes mainly from its users.

Operating system. Software that controls the computer's basic operations and flow of information.

Optical character recognition. Has two phases. Phase 1 (hardware): An optical scanner takes a picture (image) of a printed page, such as a contract or a deed. Phase 2 (software): An OCR program uses image pattern-recognition techniques to convert the image into text readable by software such as a word processor.

Optical disk drive. Direct access disk written and read by light. Has huge storage capacity but is expensive. Also known as "WORM" drives ("Write Once, Read Many") because information can only be recorded once on it, but retrieved ad infinitum.

Output device. A device, such as a monitor or printer, that gets information out of a computer.

Pattern matching. You use pattern matching to locate text in a document. For example, with a search for "homicid*", you can find all occurrences of homicidal, homicide, and homisides in a deposition. The asterisk in "homicid*" is a wildcard character.

Pattern recognition. Computer analysis of an image for recognizable written characters; computer analysis of a voice recording for recognizable spoken words.

PCMCIA card. A removable card for notebook and subnotebook computers. Can hold memory, modems, fax/modems, and hard disks. Not all mobile computers can use PCMCIA cards, and not all PCMCIA-enabled mobile computers can read all PCMCIA cards. (This confusion often results when an industry attempts to impose a *de jure* standard.)

PCMCIA. A consortium of mobile computer manufacturers, the Personal Computer Memory Card International Association. Informally, stands for "People Cannot Memorize Computer Industry Algorithms."

Peripheral. See hardware device.

Permanent storage. Where your electronic information lives. Electronic information remains in permanent storage whether your computer's power is on or off.

Personal information manager. Software that handles miscellaneous bits of information well: appointments, to-dos, notes to yourself.

Port. A socket on the back of a computer to which you can connect a hardware device.

Portable computer. A computer that you can carry around fairly easily.

Processor. The "brain" of a computer; does arithmetic and logical operations. Processes instructions from software.

Proprietary file format. A file format for which specifications are known only to the vendor.

RAM. See Random access memory.

Random access memory. A form of temporary storage in desktop computers. Often just called memory.

Relational database. Database with linked tables. (The complete "computer science" definition of relational databases is much more complex than this.)

Root directory. The highest-level directory on a permanent storage device. Can contain files and other (sub) directories.

Sequential access. Means that a drive must search permanent storage from beginning to end to find the information it wants. A tape drive is a sequential access drive.

Shareware. Software sold on a "try it and buy it if you like it" basis.

Software. Instructions that tell a computer what to do.

Sound board. A hardware device you can use to make sound recordings on your computer and play them back. Used with both voice and music. Also called a *sound card.*

Spreadsheet program. Software to create and manipulate tables of numbers. Makes it easy to calculate and recalulate

Standard file format. A file format for which specifications are known generally.

Street price. Typical selling price for computer hardware and software.

Subnotebook computer. A type of portable computer; weighs 3 to 4 pounds and is less powerful than a notebook computer.

System board. See motherboard.

Tape. A form of permanent storage, used primarily for archiving files.

Temporary storage. The processor uses temporary storage to work on information from permanent storage. Information in temporary storage stays there as long as the computer is turned on and is lost when the computer is turned off.

Tower case. A computer case that is taller than it is wide.

Transfer rate. How fast a device transfers data to the computer.

Upload. To send a file from your computer to another computer.

User Interface. The way you interact with a computer program: the screens you see, the menus you see, the commands you give.

Utility software. Software to manipulate files, enable hardware devices to work with a computer, and perform diagnostics on a computer and its devices.

Version. Somewhat analogous to an edition of a book. A new version of software adds new features and fixes old bugs. Since 1987, WordPerfect has released versions 4.2, 5.0, 5.1, 5.2, and 6.0 of its word processing software.

Virus. A computer program that changes your computer's memory and hard disk in ways you don't want.

Voice recognition. Converts human voice into instructions a computer can recognize.

Warm boot. Restarting your computer by pressing the Ctrl-Alt-Del key combination.

Wildcard character. A special character used to represent one or more characters when doing a search.

Word processing program. Software to create and edit documents.

WORM drive. See optical disk drive.

WYSIWYG. What You See Is What You Get, pronounced "wizzy wig." WYSIWYG applications show you on screen exactly how your document will look when you print it.

About the Author

Carol Woodbury is a Chicago-based attorney and frequent writer on law and technology subjects. From 1989 to 1993 she consulted with over one thousand lawyers and other legal professionals who visited the ABA's LawTech Center in Chicago. Previously, she worked as a computer programmer/analyst for 10 years, graduated from the University of Michigan Law School in 1985, and practiced computer law in Ann Arbor, Michigan. She is currently the assistant editor of *Network 2d*, the quarterly newsletter of the ABA Section of Law Practice Management, Computer Division.

Tables and figures

Index

HP LaserJet IV, 37
HP LaserJet IVSI, 37

I

IBM, 14, 19, 38, 103
IBM-compatible, 45
IBM OS/2, 14-15, 45, 46, 105
IBM PC, *see also* PC, 104-106, 108
IBM PC/AT, 12, 104-105
IBM PC/XT, 24, 39, 104
icon, 46
images, 55-56
industry standards, 12
"Information Highway", 96
Infosources Publishing, 93
input devices, 24
input/output devices, 24
installation, 77, 117
installed user base, 78
insurance, professional liability, 3
integrated package, 84
    Microsoft Works, 84
Intel, 19, 37-38, 104
internal devices, 24
Internet, 96-97
Internet in One Day, 97

J

Jobs, Steve, 104
Juris, 85
Jurisoft, 82

K

keyboard, 15, 23, 24, 32, 38-39, 42,
    64, 99, 100, 109, 110, 112-113
key combination, 74
kilobyte (K or KB), 20

L

LAN (local area netwrok), 15, 77, 95
Lantastic, 95
laser-jet toner, 40
laser printer, 15, *see also* printer
Law Office Computing, 74
Law Practice Management
    Magazine, 73
The Lawyer's PC, 74, 83
leasing, 39
Leder's Legal Tech Newsletter, 74

LEXIS, 19, 54, 65, 95, 96, 97
license agreements, 106-107
Linkskys, 93
list price, 36
LitApps, 74
Locate 1993-1994, 73
look-up (pop-up) tables, 76
Lotus, 83
Lotus Agenda, 12, 14
Lotus AmiPro, 82
Lotus Approach, 66
Lotus Development Corp., 12
Lotus Organizer, 68

M

Macintosh, *see* Apple Macintosh
magnetic tape drive, 23, 24, 25, 116-
    117
magnetic tapes, 21, 23, 24, 25, 112,
    116-117
mail order catalogs, listed, 40-41
mainframe computers, 103-104
malfunctions, 118
Management Information Systems
    Dept., (MIS), 104
Matthew Bender, 93
MECA Software, Inc., 85
Megabyte (MB), 20
MegaHertz (MHz), defined, 19
memory cache, 21
memory manager program, 15
menus, 46, 47, 74, 76, 101
Microsoft Access, 66
Microsoft Corporation, 45, 83, 105-
    106
Microsoft Publisher, 83
Microsoft video clip, 26
Microsoft Windows, 13, 14, 20, 21,
    27, 38, 43, 45, 46-47, 49, 51, 55, 56,
    57, 65, 71, 75, 79, 81, 82, 85, 92, 94,
    97, 100, 101, 105-106, 115, 116, 117,
    118, 119
Microsoft Windows for Workgroups,
    95
Microsoft Windows NT, 105
Microsoft Word, 3, 50, 102
    for Windows, 57, 82, 83, 117, 118
Microsoft Works, 84
millisecond (ms), 24

R

RAM (random access memory), 21
RAM-cram, 105
root directory, 49

S

scanner, *see* optical scanner
screen, *see* monitor
screen saver, 110
SCSI hard disk drive, 41, 110
search and retreival, 54, 55
sequential access drive, 23
serial cable, 25
serial mouse, 25
shareware, 96
small label printer, 25
Smartdrive, 116
SneakerNet, 93
Soft Solutions, 83, 92
software, computer
  bankruptcy, 66, 70, 92
  bookkeeping, 85
    QuickBooks for Windows, 85
    TaxCut '93 for Windows by
      MECA Software, 85
  bugs, 12, 76, 117-118
  case management, 79, 86
  copy-protected, 77-78
  custom database, 79
  defined, 10
  demo disk, 75
  docket control, 66, 70, 71, 73, 76,
    77, 78, 79, 86, 91
  dongles, 78
  estate planning, 66, 92
  evaluation copy, 75
  fax, 97
  integrated legal market, 70-71, 78-
    79
  legal market, 16, 50, 54, 66, 68-71,
    73-79, 85, 92
  litigation support, 70, 91-92
  mass-market, 16, 54, 66, 68-71, 73-
    79, 81-82, 84-85, 86, 91-92
  off-the-shelf, 16, 20, 65, 75, 79
  real estate, 92
  spreadsheets, 15, 16, 46, 47, 54,
    58, 83, 84, 91, 92, 101, 104, 108
  substantive, 92

time/billing, 53, 54, 66, 70, 71, 73,
  75, 77, 78, 79, 84-85, 95
    Juris, 85
    One-Write Plus Accounting
      from Business Services
      Software, Inc., 85
      Software Technology, Inc., 85
      Timeslips for Windows by
        Timeslips Corp., 85
  versions, 12
Software Technology, Inc., 85
sound board, 26, 57
Stac Technologies, 116
stacker, 116
standard file formats, 50
street price, 36
subnotebook computer, 27
Sybex, 101
system board, *see* motherboard

T

tables, 58-59, 61-71, 76-77
tape drives, *see* magnetic tape drives
tapes, *see* magnetic tapes
TaxCut '93 for Windows, 85
technical support, 12, 96, 109, 110
temporary storage, 21, 22, 23
terminal, 97
TimeSlips Corp., 85
TimeSlips for Windows, 85
trade magazines, 10-11, 14, 17, 37,
  73-74, 75, 78, 103
transfer rate, 24

U

upgrades, 32, 109, 117-118
upload, 96
user interface, 46, 76
utility programs, 50, 91

V

viruses, 117, 118
VisiCalc, 104
voice recognition, 54, 57-58, 64, 100

W

warm boot, 118
warranty, 41-42, 109, 112
West, 93

Selected Books From...

THE SECTION OF LAW PRACTICE MANAGEMENT

ABA Guide to International Business Negotiations. A guide to the general, legal, and cultural issues that arise during international negotiations. Details negotiation issues within 17 countries.

ACCESS 1994. An updated guidebook to technology resources. Includes practical hints, practical tips, commonly used terms, and resource information.

Breaking Traditions. A guide to progressive, flexible, and sensible work alternatives for lawyers who want to balance the demand of the legal profession with other commitments. Model policy for childbirth and parenting leave is included.

Changing Jobs, 2nd Ed. A handbook designed to help lawyers make changes in their professional careers. Includes career planning advice from nearly 50 experts.

Flying Solo: A Survival Guide for the Solo Lawyer, 2nd Ed. An updated and expanded guide to the problems and issues unique to the solo practitioner.

How to Start and Build a Law Practice, 3rd Ed. Jay Foonberg's classic guide has been updated and expanded. Included are more than 10 new chapters on marketing, financing, automation, practicing from home, ethics and professional responsibility.

Last Frontier: Women Lawyers as Rainmakers. Explains why rainmaking is different for women than men and focuses on ways to improve these skills. Shares the experiences of four women who have successfully built their own practices.

Law Office Staff Manual, 2nd Ed. This updated version includes new sections on sexual harassment, alternative work schedules, and attorney publicity. Also includes the text of the manual on diskettes in WordPerfect and ASCII formats so that you can create a customized manual for your law firm.

Leveraging with Legal Assistants. Reviews the changes that have led to increased use of legal assistants and the need to enlarge their role further. Learn specific ways in which a legal assistant can handle a substantial portion of traditional lawyer work.

Making Partner: A Guide for Law Firm Associates. Written by a managing partner, this book offers guidelines and recommendations designed to help you increase your chances of making partner.

Planning the Small Law Office Library. A step-by-step guide to planning, building, and managing a small law office library. Includes case studies, floor plans, and questionnaires.

Practical Systems: Tips for Organizing Your Law Office. It will help you get control of your in-box by outlining systems for managing daily work.

Results-Oriented Financial Management: A Guide to Successful Law Firm Financial Performance. How to manage "the numbers," from setting rates and computing billable hours to calculating net income and preparing the budget. Over 30 charts and statements to help you prepare reports.

A Short Course in Personal Computers. Explains the basic components of IBM-compatible computers in terms that are easy to understand. This concise and accessible guide will help you make knowledgeable decisions in the law office.

Survival Skills for the Practicing Lawyer. Includes 29 articles from *Law Practice Management* magazine for the attorney with little or no management responsibilities.

Through the Client's Eyes: New Approaches to Get Clients to Hire You Again and Again. Includes an overview of client relations and sample letters, surveys, and self-assessment questions to gauge your client relations acumen.

The Time Trap. A classic book on time management published by the American Management Association. This guide focuses on "The Twenty Biggest Time Wasters" and how you can overcome them.

TQM in Action: One Firm's Journey Toward Quality and Excellence. A guide to implementing the principles of Total Quality Management in your law firm.

When a Professional Divorces. Discusses how to value a professional license and practice when a lawyer or other professional divorces.

Winning with Computers, Part 1. Addresses virtually every aspect of the use of computers in litigation. You'll get an overview of products available and tips on how to put them to good use. For the beginning and advanced computer user.

Winning with Computers, Part 2. Expands on the ways you can use computers to manage the routine and not-so-routine aspects of your trial practice. Learn how to apply general purpose software and even how to have fun with your computer.

Win-Win Billing Strategies. Represents the first comprehensive analysis of what constitutes "value," and how to bill for it. You'll learn how to initiate and implement different billing methods that make sense for you and your client.

Women Rainmakers' 101+ Best Marketing Tips. A collection of over 130 marketing tips suggested by women rainmakers throughout the country. Includes tips on image, networking, public relations, and advertising.

WordPerfect® in One Hour for Lawyers. This is a crash course in the most popular word processing software package used by lawyers. In four easy lessons, you'll learn the basic steps for getting a simple job done.

WordPerfect® Shortcuts for Lawyers: Learning Merge and Macros in One Hour. A fast-track guide to two of WordPerfect's more advanced functions: merge and macros. Includes 4 lessons designed to take 15 minutes each.

Your New Lawyer, 2nd Ed. A complete legal employer's guide to recruitment, development, and management of new lawyers. Updated to address the many changes in the practice of law since the 1983 edition.

Order Form

Qty	Title	LPM Price	Regular Price	Total
_____	ABA Guide to Int'l Business Negotiations (511-0331)	$74.95	$84.95	$_____
_____	ACCESS 1994 (511-0327)	29.95	34.95	$_____
_____	Breaking Traditions (511-0320)	64.95	74.95	$_____
_____	Changing Jobs, 2nd Ed. (511-0334)	49.95	59.95	$_____
_____	Flying Solo, 2nd Ed. (511-0328)	59.95	69.95	$_____
_____	How to Start & Build a Law Practice, 3rd Ed. (511-0293)	32.95	39.95	$_____
_____	Last Frontier (511-0314)	9.95	14.95	$_____
_____	Law Office Staff Manual (511-0307)	79.00	89.00	$_____
_____	Leveraging with Legal Assistants (511-0322)	59.95	69.95	$_____
_____	Making Partner (511-0303)	14.95	19.95	$_____
_____	Planning the Small Law Office Library (511-0325)	29.95	39.95	$_____
_____	Practical Systems (511-0296)	24.95	34.95	$_____
_____	Results-Oriented Financial Management (511-0319)	44.95	54.95	$_____
_____	A Short Course in Personal Computers (511-0302)	14.95	24.95	$_____
_____	Survival Skills for the Practicing Lawyer (511-0324)	39.95	49.95	$_____
_____	Through the Client's Eyes (511-0337)	69.95	79.95	$_____
_____	The Time Trap (511-0330)	14.95	14.95	$_____
_____	TQM in Action (511-0323)	59.95	69.95	$_____
_____	When a Professional Divorces (511-0326)	49.95	59.95	$_____
_____	Winning with Computers, Part 1 (511-0294)	89.95	99.95	$_____
_____	Winning with Computers, Part 2 (511-0315)	59.95	69.95	$_____
_____	Winning with Computers, Parts 1 & 2 (511-0316)	124.90	144.90	$_____
_____	Win-Win Billing Strategies (511-0304)	89.95	99.95	$_____
_____	Women Rainmakers' 101+ Best Marketing Tips (511-0336)	14.95	19.95	$_____
_____	WordPerfect® in One Hour for Lawyers (511-0308)	9.95	14.95	$_____
_____	WordPerfect® Shortcuts for Lawyers (511-0329)	14.95	19.95	$_____
_____	Your New Lawyer, 2nd Ed. (511-0312)	74.95	84.95	$_____

* HANDLING	** TAX
$2.00-$9.99.........$2.00	DC residents add 5.75%
10.00-24.99.........$3.95	IL residents add 8.75%
25.00-49.99.........$4.95	MD residents add 5%
50.00 +...............$5.95	

SUBTOTAL: $_____

*HANDLING: $_____

**TAX: $_____

TOTAL: $_____

PAYMENT

☐ Check enclosed (Payable to the ABA)   ☐ Bill Me

☐ Visa   ☐ MasterCard   Account Number: _____-_____-_____-_____

Exp. Date: _____ Signature _____

Name _____

Firm _____

Address _____

City_____State_____ZIP _____

Phone number_____

Mail to: ABA, Publication Orders, P.O. Box 10892, Chicago, IL 60610-0892

PHONE: (312) 988-5522
Or FAX: (312) 988-5568

BOOK

THE SECTION OF
LAW PRACTICE
MANAGEMENT

CUSTOMER COMMENT FORM

Title of Book: _____

We've tried to make this publication as useful, accurate, and readable as possible. Please take 5 minutes to tel us if we succeeded. Your comments and suggestions will help us improve our publications. Thank you!

1. How did you acquire this publication:

☐ by mail order ☐ at a meeting/convention ☐ as a gift

☐ by phone order ☐ at a bookstore ☐ don't know

☐ other: (describe) _____

Please rate this publication as follows:

	Excellent	Good	Fair	Poor	Not Applicable
Readability: Was the book easy to read and understand?	☐	☐	☐	☐	☐
Examples/Cases: Were they helpful, practical? Were there enough?	☐	☐	☐	☐	☐
Content: Did the book meet your expectations? Did it cover the subject adequately?	☐	☐	☐	☐	☐
Organization and clarity: Was the sequence of text logical? Was it easy to find what you wanted to know?	☐	☐	☐	☐	☐
Illustrations/forms/checklists: Were they clear and useful? Were there enough?	☐	☐	☐	☐	☐
Physical attractiveness: What did you think of the appearance of the publication (typesetting, printing, etc.)?	☐	☐	☐	☐	☐

Would you recommend this book to another attorney/administrator? ☐ Yes ☐ No

How could this publication be improved? What else would you like to see in it?

_____

_____

_____

Do you have other comments or suggestions? _____

_____

Name _____

Firm/Company _____

Address _____

City/State/Zip _____

Phone _____

Firm Size: _____ Area of specialization: _____

We appreciate your time and help.

Fold

BUSINESS REPLY MAIL

FIRST CLASS   PERMIT NO. 16471   CHICAGO, ILLINOIS

POSTAGE WILL BE PAID BY ADDRESSEE

AMERICAN BAR ASSOCIATION
PPM, 8th FLOOR
750 N. LAKE SHORE DRIVE
CHICAGO, ILLINOIS 60611-9851

Fold